100
Poems
to Save
the
Earth

100
Poems
to Save
the
Earth

Edited by Zoë Brigley & Kristian Evans

SEREN

Seren is the book imprint of
Poetry Wales Press Ltd.
Suite 6, 4 Derwen Road, Bridgend, Wales, CF31 1LH
www.serenbooks.com
facebook.com / SerenBooks
twitter@SerenBooks

Introduction © Kristian Evans & Zoë Brigley, 2021
Poems & Prose © individual authors

ISBN: 978-1-78172-624-2

A CIP record for this title is available from the British Library.

The publisher acknowledges the financial assistance of
the Books Council of Wales.

Cover artwork: Sequoia Piece, Canada 2012, Pigment print 150 x 150 cm
by NILS-UDO, Courtesy Galerie Pierre-Alain Challier, Paris

Printed by Bell & Bain Ltd, Glasgow.

CONTENTS

INTRODUCTION

The title of this anthology is provocatively posed, not to make any grand claims, but to emphasize that the earth is on the brink of catastrophic change. It could not be more important for poets to address this startling fact.

The reader might well ask, how *can* poems save the earth? Certainly not by marching in step with political campaigns, diverting poetry's meander into propaganda's mill (no matter how worthwhile the cause might seem). What is "earth" after all? Isn't it our shared ground, beyond all claim of border and boundary? A ground we share not only with fellow humans, but with those who are *more-than-human*, to borrow from David Abrams, or indeed, to look to older indigenous traditions. The insects, birds, mammals, rivers, mountains, bushfires, ocean currents — are they persons too? Poetry invites us to fine-tune our senses, to pay attention, to feel more carefully for the pulse of things. It asks us to slow down and notice what we have been missing, to remember what we have forgotten.

As William Blake puts it: "The tree which moves some to tears of joy is in the eyes of others only a green thing that stands in the way." Our crisis is fundamentally a crisis of perception. Where one person sees the earth as an inert heap of resources to be exploited, another will see a living web of connections and relationships, the complexity of which is often beyond our ability to understand. Blake concludes: "to the eyes of the man of imagination, nature is imagination itself." Too often it seems the earth is a mirror, in which we find only ourselves. What else is out there? Can we find the words to describe it, to share it, to *share with it*?

Such questions and concerns as these are increasingly to be found at the heart of contemporary poetry. And by that we mean *all* poetry. In finding poems for this anthology, we have abandoned a traditional view of "nature poetry" or "environmental" writing, especially where it side-lines particular groups (e.g. people of the global majority/BAME/BIPOC writers, LGBTQ+ poets, or writers with disabilities).

Indeed, the voices gathered here often speak in terms of ecological justice, noting the connections between the exploitation of the environment and inequalities experienced by groups allowed fewer privileges. They implicitly and explicitly question what nature means, what the earth is, what our relations are and what they may yet become. Old certainties have been eroded by new circumstances. These poems absorb the changes, compost the waste, redraw the maps and, full of trust, keep going.

We live in a time of unprecedented crisis, of mass extinction, accumulations of alarming data, and terrifying predictions. Increasingly, people are suffering from eco-anxiety and eco-grief as the bleak enormity of our situation sinks in. It often seems easier and better to close our eyes, to sleep and forget. A million ingenious distractions are just a click away, waiting to deliver a lullaby. Poetry however calls us to stay awake, to find the words to describe how it feels, to sing to what hurts, to reach out, to attend more closely and with more care, to each other, and to our fellow species, to see all things as our kin. In fact, it may be that poetry is exactly what we need to save the earth.

Kristian Evans & Zoë Brigley

Kathleen Jamie

THE CREEL

The world began with a woman,
shawl-happed, stooped under a creel,
whose slow step you recognize
from troubled dreams. You feel

obliged to help bear her burden
from hill or kelp-strewn shore,
but she passes by unseeing
thirled to her private chore.

It's not sea birds or peat she's carrying,
not fleece, nor the herring bright
but her fear that if ever she put it down
the world would go out like a light.

Roger Robinson

A PORTABLE PARADISE

And if I speak of Paradise,
then I'm speaking of my grandmother
who told me to carry it always
on my person, concealed, so
no one else would know but me.
That way they can't steal it, she'd say.
And if life puts you under pressure,
trace its ridges in your pocket,
smell its piney scent on your handkerchief,
hum its anthem under your breath.
And if your stresses are sustained and daily,
get yourself to an empty room — be it hotel,
hostel or hovel — find a lamp
and empty your paradise onto a desk:
your white sands, green hills and fresh fish.
Shine the lamp on it like the fresh hope
of morning, and keep staring at it till you sleep.

David Morley

CHORUS

on the birth of Edward Daniel Keenan Morley

The song-thrush slams down gauntlets on its snail-anvil.
The nightjar murmurs in nightmare. The dawn is the chorus.
The bittern blasts the mists wide with a booming foghorn.
The nuthatch nails another hatch shut. The dawn is the chorus.
The merlin bowls a boomerang over bracken then catches it.
The capercaillie uncorks its bottled throat. The dawn is the chorus.
The treecreeper tips the trees upside down to trick out insects.
The sparrow sorts spare parts on a pavement. The dawn is the chorus.
The hoopoe hoops rainbows over the heath and hedgerows.
The wren runs rings through its throat. The dawn is the chorus.
The turnstones do precisely what is asked of them by name.
The wryneck and stonechats also. The dawn is the chorus.
The buzzards mew and mount up on the thermal's thermometer.
The smew slide on shy woodland water. The dawn is the chorus.
The heron hangs its head before hurling down its guillotine.
The tern twists on tines of two sprung wings. The dawn is the chorus.
The eider shreds its pillows, releases snow flurry after snow flurry.
The avocet unclasps its compass-points. The dawn is the chorus.
The swallow unmakes the Spring and names the Summer.
The swift sleeps only when it's dead. The dawn is the chorus.
The bullfinches feather-fight the birdbath into a bloodbath.
The wagtail wags a wand then vanishes. The dawn is the chorus.
The corncrake zips its comb on its expert fingertip.
The robin blinks at you for breakfast. The dawn is the chorus.
The rook roots into roadkill for the heart and the hardware.
The tawny owl wakes us to our widowhood. The dawn is the chorus.
The dawn is completely composed. The pens of its beaks are dry.
Day will never sound the same, nor night know which song wakes her.

Gbenga Adesina

GLORY

Glory of plums, femur of Glory.
Glory of ferns
on a dark platter.

Glory of willows, Glory of Stag beetles
Glory of the long obedience
of the kingfisher.

Glory of waterbirds, Glory
of thirst.

Glory of the Latin
of the dead and their grammar
composed entirely of decay.

Glory of the eyes of my father
which, when he died, closed
inside his grave,

and opened even more brightly
inside me.

Glory of dark horses
running furiously
inside their own

dark horses.

Carl Phillips

MONOMOY

Somewhere, people must still do things like fetch
water from wells in buckets, then pour it out
for those animals that, long domesticated, would
likely perish before figuring out how to get
for themselves. That dog, for example, whose
refusal to leave my side I mistook, as a child,
for loyalty — when all along it was just blind ... What
is it about vulnerability that can make the hand
draw back, sometimes, and can sometimes seem
the catalyst for rendering the hand into sheer force,
destructive? *Don't you see how you've burnt almost*
all of it, all the tenderness, away, someone screams
to someone else, in public — and looking elsewhere,
we walk quickly past, as if even to have heard
that much might have put us at risk of whatever fate
questions like that
                              spring from. Estrangement —
like sacrifice — begins as a word at first, soon it's
the stuff of drama, cue the follow-up tears that
attend drama, then it's pretty much the difference
between waking up to a storm and waking up
inside one. Who can say how she got there —
in the ocean, I mean — but I once watched a horse
make her way back to land mid-hurricane: having
ridden, surfer-like, the very waves that at any moment
could have overwhelmed her in their crash to shore, she
shook herself, looked back once on the water's restlessness —
history's always restless — and the horse stepped free.

Camille T. Dungy

TROPHIC CASCADE

After the reintroduction of gray wolves
to Yellowstone and, as anticipated, their culling
of deer, trees grew beyond the deer stunt
of the midcentury. In their up reach
songbirds nested, who scattered
seed for underbrush, and in that cover
warrened snowshoe hare. Weasel and water shrew
returned, also vole, and came soon hawk
and falcon, bald eagle, kestrel, and with them
hawk shadow, falcon shadow. Eagle shade
and kestrel shade haunted newly berried
runnels where mule deer no longer rummaged, cautious
as they were, now, of being surprised by wolves. Berries
brought bear, while undergrowth and willows, growing
now right down to the river, brought beavers,
who dam. Muskrats came to the dams, and tadpoles.
Came, too, the night song of the fathers
of tadpoles. With water striders, the dark
gray American dipper bobbed in fresh pools
of the river, and fish stayed, and the bear, who
fished, also culled deer fawns and to their kill scraps
came vulture and coyote, long gone in the region
until now, and their scat scattered seed, and more
trees, brush, and berries grew up along the river
that had run straight and so flooded but thus dammed,
compelled to meander, is less prone to overrun. Don't
you tell me this is not the same as my story. All this
life born from one hungry animal, this whole,
new landscape, the course of the river changed,
I know this. I reintroduced myself to myself, this time
a mother. After which, nothing was ever the same.

Clare Pollard

IN THE HORNIMAN MUSEUM

In South London, on a Sunday,
we have seen the scratching chickens
and alpacas being spitty
when the rain drives us indoors
where the taxidermy's waiting
and you race around glass coffins,
the hummingbirds in friezes,
Vulpes vulpes and the *Cervus*
posed like toys in toyshop windows
and the walrus like a punchline.
They are animals, as you are —
relation of *Pan troglodytes* —
each captured by a caption
in a tea trader's collection.
He paid to have the world paused:
all those thousand conscious seeings
for one vision! All that *I am*
turned to glaze for one man's gaze.

I've not told you about death yet.
Can you tell these birds are different?
Do you think this heron cruel,
that he doesn't care about you?
It's true. The heron doesn't.
Caring's something rare and fleeting
(if the dead see anything
then it's as hard and black as glass.)
But your eyes are getting rounder,
pointing 'dere!' at crocs and gibbons
and the peacock's staring blueness,
and we're falling through our days
in this pissing useless ark
while the clouds gather like stuffing,
while the water's ticking upwards.

My child you are an *I*.
Through your two eyes, not yet dark,
can you see your wet-cheeked mother
and the whole creaturely Kingdom
as they stand today before you
in their opulence and armour,
who have held their breath this moment
and are waiting for your judgement?

Craig Santos Perez

(FIRST TRIMESTER)

[we] are watching a documentary about home
birth when [you] first feel [neni] kick / / embryo

of hope / / they say plastic is the perfect creation
because it never dies / / litters the beaches

of o'ahu, this "gathering place" / / the doctor
recommends a c-section / / in the sea, plastic multiplies

into smaller pieces, leaches estrogenic and toxic
chemicals / / if [we] cut open the bellies of whales

and large fish, what fragments will [we] find, derived
from oil, absorbed into tissue / / because plastic

never dissolves, every product ever made still exists,
somewhere, today / / i wish my daughter was made

of plastic so that she will survive [our] wasteful
hands / / so that she, too, will have a great future

W.S. Graham

I LEAVE THIS AT YOUR EAR

For Nessie Dunsmuir

I leave this at your ear for when you wake,
A creature in its abstract cage asleep.
Your dreams blindfold you by the light they make.

The owl called from the naked-woman tree
As I came down by the Kyle farm to hear
Your house silent by the speaking sea.

I have come late but I have come before
Later with slaked steps from stone to stone
To hope to find you listening for the door.

I stand in the ticking room. My dear, I take
A moth kiss from your breath. The shore gulls cry.
I leave this at your ear for when you wake.

John Burnside

EARTH

David 'Gypsy' Chain, killed while protesting the clearcutting of California Redwoods, Humboldt County, September 1998

Too late to say it aloud, but what I love
are phantom birds and girls with parasols

in paintings that no one looks at any more, the breathless
quiet of *pentimenti* sealed in the pigment;

and every living thing that went extinct
before a man could name it, unknown

hummingbirds and tree frogs, fig-trees, orchids,
aeons of filmy fern gone down to coal, lost

redwoods veined with centuries of light
and the faint but indelible stain of a living man

who died because he trusted to the earth
the heart he had kept intact, though no one in these parts

speaks any longer of hearts, or the sound in the trees
that once was a spirit and now is no more than the wind.

Vidyan Ravinthiran

MORE CONTEXT REQUIRED

There is no clear picture as yet
as to how many tigers were killed or if they were blue
because it's that
time of year and they did themselves in as you do.
I have been becoming more
and more independent but I'm not a journalist
or the kind of guy asked if I know the score
now it's hard to remember even if we won or lost,
and who we are exactly. There was
a protest, I remember that, and stories
about women and children
that somehow became about a witch and her cauldron,
or how exactly the tiger got his stripes.
And beautiful computer-generated maps.

Pascale Petit

FOR A COMING EXTINCTION

(after W. S. Merwin)

You whom we have named Charger, Challenger,
Great King, and Noor the shining one,

now that you are at the brink of extinction,
I am writing to those of you

who have reached the black groves of the sky,
where you glide beneath branches of galaxies,

your fur damasked with constellations,
tell him who sits at the centre of the mystery,

that we did all we could.
That we kept some of you alive

in the prisons we built for you.
You tigers of Amur and Sumatra,

of Turkey and Iran, Java and Borneo,
and you — Royal Bengals, who lingered last.

Tell the one who would judge
that we are innocent of your slaughter.

That we kiss each pugmark,
the water trembling inside

as if you had just passed.
Masters of ambush and camouflage,

hiding behind astral trees,
invisible as always,

when we gaze up at the night,
when we look lightyears into the past —

we see your eyes staring down at us.

Carrie Etter

KARNER BLUE

*"a place called Karner, where in some pine barrens, on lupines,
a little blue butterfly I have described and named ought to be out."*
                                        Vladimir Nabokov

Because it used to be more populous in Illinois.
Because its wingspan is an inch.
Because it requires blue lupine.
Because to become blue, it has to ingest the leaves of a blue plant.
Because its scientific name, *Lycaeides melissa samuelis*, is mellifluous.
Because the female is not only blue but blue and orange and silver
        and black.
Because its beauty galvanizes collectors.
Because Nabokov named it.
Because its collection is criminal.
Because it lives in black oak savannahs and pine barrens.
Because it once produced landlocked seas.
Because it has declined ninety per cent in fifteen years.
Because it is.

Carter Revard

OVER BY FAIRFAX, LEAVING TRACKS

For Mike and Casey and the Kids

The storm's left
this fresh blue sky, over
Salt Creek running brown
and quick, and a huge tiger
swallowtail tasting the brilliant
orange flowers beside our trail.
Lightning and thunder've spread
a clean sheet of water over
these last-night possum tracks
straight-walking like a dinosaur in
the mud, and next to these we've
left stippled tracks from soles made
in Hong Kong, maybe with Osage oil.
Lawrence and Wesley pick blue-speckled flints
along our path, one Ponca boy
in braids, one part Osage
in cowboy hat.
Over the blue Pacific, green Atlantic we
have come together here; possum's
the oldest furred being in this New World,
we're newest in his Old World.
Far older, though,
and younger too, the tiger swallowtail has
gone sailing from those orange flowers to
sky-blue nectar: the wild morning
glories
will spring up where she's touched, marking
her next year's trail.
Makes me wonder,
if archaeologists should ever dig those prints
with possum's here, whether they'll see
the winged beings who moved
in brightness near us, leaving no tracks except
in flowers and
these winged words.

The Cyborg Jillian Weise

BODY AS CLOUD

Before the body there were photographs
        of the body, gray transparent clouds.
The parents saw fists the size of hail
        and this meant confidence in her walk.
The doctor saw heart and lungs, skull
        and brain; this was all good,
no need to test for Down Syndrome
        or others because the cloud was big
and full. The cloud was yawning, breathing.
        When the body came out twisted, six toes
on one foot, a club foot, no tibia,
        no fibula, lungs trapped by the rib cage
what explanations could be given
        more than why we see clouds differently?
Why some are rabbit ears
        while others are the tails of lions?

Isabel Galleymore

LIMPET & DRILL-TONGUED WHELK

Across the rockpool floor, a limpet grazes —
a stray magician's cup,
moon-textured, the shape of light
pointing through frosted glass.
It is a modest party hat
in which something like a head resides
oblivious of this dog whelk
that pads against the thick, still brine
and climbs upon the limpet —
an ornate seat upon an elephant.
Carnivorous mollusc, tiny fracking rig
clocking in with its drill-tongue, clutching
as the limpet rises from the stone,
to become half-mushroom, half bucking bronco.

Maggie Wang

THE SUN ON THE TIP OF
A SNAIL'S SHELL

picture the eggs buried in the dirt you have taken
from the shade of the trees in o'ahu where you

found the snails all those years ago. picture them
murky like the brackish sea after a storm, not

blinding the sunlight back into the undersides
of the leaves or the eyes of those snails, darting

from branch to branch, sharpened on genealogies
you will never understand. picture them hatching

like the half-moon on the incoming tide, and
think how you will keep them alive, delicate

creatures not cut for winds as harsh as those
raging outside. picture their shells hardening

into the colour of pineapples or the rose-gold
teeth of some foreign beast, not knowing the

difference between them. picture them crushing
the last of the moss beneath their feet—the moss

you have gathered, too, from those trees—not
realizing they have never lived in the wild, not

answering to the names you have given them, not
understanding they are the last of their kind.

Marvin Thompson

WHILST SEARCHING FOR ANANSI WITH MY MIXED RACE CHILDREN IN THE BLAEN BRAN COMMUNITY WOODLAND

1.

A fox lies still by a birch. 'Dad, is it dead?'
asks Derys. Crouching down, I watch an ant
crawl through its ear-fur. Inside my head

are Mark Duggan's smile and last night's heavy dread:
I dreamt his death again. A distant love
once stroked my cheek and said: *'They shot him dead*

only because he had a gun.' I still see red
and white carnations; a girl who now frequents
her father's grave; brown birch leaves descending

a walk to school. '85. Mum's palm bled
sweat, Tottenham's air strangely grey. Stagnant.
We passed my friend's burnt front door — flames had fed

on parked cars. In tower blocks, rage had spread
like an Arab Spring: numbing unemployment,
the oppressive use of sus laws. *'Is my friend dead?'*

Mum answered with silence. Hunkered on mud,
my prayer withers, the birch's leaves hang slant
and noonlight shrouds the fox. 'Sorry. It's dead.'
'It's breathing, Dad,' shouts Hayden. 'Listen, hard!'

2.

Crouched by the fox's nose, I listen
to placate my son. The fox is breathing.
Should I leave it here to die? Its fur glistens

with drizzle — each breath makes my eyes moisten
as though a gospel singer's voice is rising
from the fox's lungs. Derys blurts, 'Dad, listen,

it needs a vet!' In the dream, Mark Duggan
lay on the Gold Coast's shore, smoke soaring
above ancestors whose dark necks glistened,

chains ready on docked ships from London.
I woke, limbs tensed, ancestors' rage jumping
in my blood, the humid night laden

with sailors' screams: 'Masts ablaze!' Will Britain
learn to love my children's melanin?
With their voices ('Yellow bird, high up...') swelling,

I carry the limp fox. The grey mountains
are watching us. A buzzard's circling.

I scratch and scratch my wrists. The vet stiffens,
holding her stethoscope. The fox's eyes listen.

Ross Gay

A SMALL NEEDFUL FACT

Is that Eric Garner worked
for some time for the Parks and Rec.
Horticultural Department, which means,
perhaps, that with his very large hands,
perhaps, in all likelihood,
he put gently into the earth
some plants which, most likely,
some of them, in all likelihood,
continue to grow, continue
to do what such plants do, like house
and feed small and necessary creatures,
like being pleasant to touch and smell,
like converting sunlight
into food, like making it easier
for us to breathe.

Kazim Ali

CHECKPOINT

"I do not know" is stamped indelibly on my passport so I am marked always for further interrogation.

Adam, named for the first man, asks me again and again, "What are you doing in our country?"

I tell him, "My intention was to go to the city called Hill of Spring and paint my nails gold."

Risen again from the ocean floor the rocks declare a state of emergency.

He asks me again and again as if my answer would change, so each time I try to change it.

"I come to dress myself in the salt of the sunken sea."

Pine nuts rain down from the outraged trees.

"I come to write my name down in the peals of bells sealed in a crease of the still-fallen wall."

The army has learned twenty-six different words for "no."

Wild fires leap from tree to tree.

Water shrinks back from its table in shame.

Kelli Russell Agodon

WHAT I CALL EROSION

Today's sea seems tired of stealing
acres of sand from the beach.
What I call erosion, the waves call:
I wish the wind would stop rushing us,
I wish we could just take it slow.

In the beauty of whitecaps, I sometimes
see sadness, sometimes how lucky we are
to watch the sunrise one more time.

There's so much we're carrying these days—
the seabirds drop another clam shell on shore,
a killdeer runs across the dunes
trying to distract everyone from its nest.

Danger, even when it's not, is everywhere.
Sometimes I pretend to have a broken wing
as I look out my window. But then a cloudscape
in a world of buffleheads, of saltwater roses,

and I forget fear. It's 7 a.m. on a Thursday
and an otter is pretending none of my concerns
matter. The otter, a sort of mad hatter,
is diving in and out of the waves, playful.

When the planet says, *This is impossible,*
the otter responds, *Only if you believe it.*

Marianne Boruch

THE OCTOPUS

fragile. Enraged.
Or terrified at the touch, pulling back,

given the no room in there, rock
on three sides, out of bay and sun,
low tide Alaska near Homer.

So hallucinate high tide where all of it

floats the life of free water
released, let go, soft underbelly of leathery
sea stars twisting how Picasso
did his nudes crazy-pitched in bad dream.

I'm told the world goes under to nothing it was.

The octopus sees us as a shadow, feels us as
feelers, the octopus
wraps and wraps in there, all arms and too many.

A hole, a rock wherein lies an eye of sorts.

Think the moment the octopus found
this place to tangle up.
Think: fear means a desperate
solace somewhere, like—

until *like* is a hook, a click
to the past wired up as right now
out of whole cloth ago,

the accident that time, the wait
in the car's swollen dark...

And I pictured my bed, my bed, my bed.

Tishani Doshi

SELF

And when they ask, what kind of animal
would you be, I always say gazelle or lark,
never cockroach, even though they'll outlast
us all. Once I dreamed I had a body with two
heads like those ancient figures from the Zarqa
River — bitumen eyes, trunks of reed and hydrated
lime, built thick and flat without genitals, nothing
shameful to eject except tears. We all want to be
monuments but can't help shoving our fingers
in dirt. Imagine a life in childhood—one face
to the womb, another to the future. What we remember
is the road, peering through a lattice at dusk,
the trauma of burial. Will we have terracotta
armies to take us through, will we be alone
with the maggots? How good the rain is
after a failed romance. Never mind the muddy
bloomers. We are appalled by life and still,
any chance we get we emerge from the earth
like cicadas to sing and fuck for a moment
of triumph. The shock we carry is that the world
doesn't need us. Even so, we go collecting parts—
an afternoon by the sea, a game of hopping on
and off scales, nose low to the ground, looking
for that other glove to complete us.
Here I am globe, spinning planet.
Tell me why you are not astonished?

Gwen Nell Westerman

LINEAR PROCESS

Our elders say
          the universe is a
                    circle.
                              Everything
                    returns to its
          beginnings.
But where do we go
          from here?
                    Where are
                              our beginnings?
                              Our parents were stripped
                              of their parents
                              names tongues   prayers,
                              lined up for their meals
                              clothes   classes tests.
                              When it was our turn
                              to come into this world,
                              they did not know
                              what family meant
                              anymore.
                              They did not
                              know.
                              Yet even
                         from here,
                    we can
               see that the
            straightest line
         on a map
      is a
   circle.

Jen Hadfield

OUR LADY OF ISBISTER

O send me another life like this —
I want the same lochans as I had before —
the wind driving spittlestrings
to skimpy shores of dark red stone;
same hot sweet slaw
of muck and shit and trampled straw;
the chimney bubbling transparent heat;
a whirpool of Muscovey ducks;
paet-reek;
a scrambling clutch of piglet-pups;
the wet socks
slamdunked along the washing line;
the shucked wet shirts in gospel
grey and sparkling sun;
wet white bell
of an XXL tee-shirt,

                                swung

a sheepdog shouting
at my rolling tyres —
polecats, rabbits, caried byres

O send me another last life like this —

This is bliss

                      this

                              no, this

      no, this

Sascha Akhtar

THE SUFI

Surrender I, speak

a word for you

a pot on flame melts
before we eat glistening
like cherrywinter, like bootblack
I polish indefinitely

reach my dizzy head
in all its circumference, touch
choose a card
save sure till you mean it
I'll clock your time in true beads
tonight I see a crash
next morning wizard hollers

a crest-fallen face, a dust-rudder

who was there on this winter's morn
I saw snow-devils whirling
& lost myself.

wine pour backwards.

hold.

Gwyneth Lewis

PAGAN ANGEL

You ask me how it is we know
God's talking, not us. When even a stone
can photograph lilies and, as it falls,
prove that gravity's no more than speed?
When loquacious skies call
in gamma rays, radio, infra-red,
and that if we're not listening at all?

The heart's a chamber whose broody dead
stage pagan rituals. Wind blows
across stone lintels, making a tune
about absent bodies.
You ask me again:
'Where's the angel acoustic?'
My dear, the curlew. The quickening rain.

Joanna Klink

SOME FEEL RAIN

Some feel rain. Some feel the beetle startle
in its ghost-part when the bark
slips. Some feel musk. Asleep against
each other in the whiskey dark, scarcely there.
When it falls apart, some feel the moondark air
drop its motes to the patch-thick slopes of
snow. Tiny blinkings of ice from the oak,
a boot-beat that comes and goes, the line of prayer
you can follow from the dusking wind to the snowy owl
it carries. Some feel sunlight
well up in blood-vessels below the skin
and wish there had been less to lose.
Knowing how it could have been, pale maples
drowsing like a second sleep above our temperaments.
Do I imagine there is any place so safe it can't be
snapped? Some feel the rivers shift,
blue veins through soil, as if the smokestacks were a long
dream of exhalation. The lynx lets its paws
skim the ground in snow and showers.
The wildflowers scatter in warm tints until
the second they are plucked. You can wait
to scrape the ankle-burrs, you can wait until Mercury
the early star underdraws the night and its blackest
districts. And wonder. Why others feel
through coal-thick night that deeply colored garnet
star. Why sparring and pins are all you have.
Why the earth cannot make its way towards you.

Grahame Davies

PRAYER

Spirit, use me today,
not in some miracle
that would make others marvel
and would make me proud.

Not in the word of wisdom
that would stay in the mind
and make me always remembered.

Not in the heroic act
that would change the world for the better
and me for the worse.

But in the mundane miracles
of honesty and truth
that keep the sky from falling.

In the unremembered quiet words
that keep a soul on the path.

And in the unnoticed acts
that keep the world moving
slowly closer to the light.

Catríona O'Reilly

A BRIEF HISTORY OF LIGHT

And the light shineth in darkness;
and the darkness comprehended is not.

The dazzle of ocean was their first infatuation,
its starry net, and the fish that mirrored it.
They knew enough to know it was not theirs.
Over the hill a dozen furnaces glowed,
the gold gleamed that was smelted in secret,
and the trapped white light shone bitterly
at the heart of the hardest stone on earth.
But they knew enough to know it was not theirs.
Then their hoards of light grew minor,
since none could view the sun straightly,
and jealousy burned their lives to the core.
So they made a god of it, shedding glory,
shedding his light on all their arguments.
Did they know enough to know it was not theirs?
The god in his wisdom preceded them westwards,
and the forests, in whose pillared interiors
black shapes dwelled, were banished for good.
They promised an end to the primitive darkness:
soon there was nothing that was not known.
They thought: *Our light is not merely reflected —*
even the forked lightning we have braided!
And they banished the god from the light of their minds.
But they mistook the light for their knowledge of the light,
till light, and only light, was everywhere.
And they vanished in this, their last illumination,
knowing barely enough to know it was not theirs.

Robert Minhinnick

THE MAGICIAN

I hang mugwort from my mirror, he says.
To keep evil away? I suggest.
No, he smiles. Because its gold dust on the bevel pleases me.

Also, I dry mugwort in the kitchen.
To stop the quaking? I ask. The terrible tremens?
The hosts of hysteria who beset us these days?

He seems surprised. For its aroma, he says.
I prefer it to wormwood and the silver salvias.
Though savory I suppose must run it close.

Upstairs, he says, I pile up pillows stuffed with mugwort buds.
Ah, I reply. A cushion for good conscience?
To nix our nightmares, our dreams of chase,
those feverish frustrations?

No, sir. I sleep soundly. Drowsing in its down until dawn.
And here, look. It grows beside the door.
So that lust does not enter? I whisper.
That dark angel daubed with unholy dew?

Not at all, he smiles. I stand most evenings in the porch
and breathe its oil, the moon in the south
and moonlight the colour of mugwort on the surf.

But look, I say. Your garden's full of it.
Surely for potions and infusions?
To keep fleas away, and nits and gnats,
and the phantoms that would haul us to hell?

My lawn's a law unto itself, he laughs.
Though sometimes, yes, I will add it to my beer
and sit and sip and sympathise
with all who called these four walls home.

They will bury me with a bunch of mugwort
pressed into both cold hands.
Then to paradise you will go, I cry.
That I might be sweeter, he smiles, on the day my bones burn,
and my friends stand and wave farewell with a simple fern.

Erin Robinsong

LATE PRAYER

May our weapons be effective feminine inventions that like life.

May we blow up like weeds, and be medicinal and everywhere.

May the disturbed ground be our pharmacy. May the exhausted

hang out in the beautiful light. May our souls moisten and reveal us.

May our actions be deft as the inhale after a dream of suffocation.

May the oligarchs get enough to eat in their souls.

May we participate in the intelligence we're in.

May we grow into our name. May political harm

be a stench that awakens. May we not be distracted.

Let our joy repeated be power that spreads.

May our wealth be common. May oligarchs come out

of their fortresses and become psychologically well.

May their wealth be returned to the people and places.

May we shift slide rise tilt roll and twist.

May we feel the very large intimacy

And may it assist us.

Michael Symmons Roberts

A NEW SONG

Sing a new song to the Lord,
sing through the skin of your teeth,
sing in the code of your blood,
sing with a throat full of earth,

sing to the quick of your nails,
sing from the knots of your lungs,
sing like a dancer on coals,
sing as a madman in tongues,

sing as if singing made sense,
sing in the caves of your heart,
sing like you want them to dance,
sing through the shades of your past,

sing what you never could say,
sing at the fulcrum of joy,
sing without need of reply.

Sean Bonney

OUR DEATH / WHAT IF THE SUMMER NEVER ENDS

None of us have slept for a long time. How could we. There were fires
up and down the Charing Cross Road. Mumbled conversations about
Apartheid. England was damp, was possibly leaking. We followed tiny
trails of liquid waste across the city. Called it aesthetics. Called it action.
We all fell down. Some of us voted. Some of us put on balaclavas. There
were several earthquakes. Endless strategies of tedious indifference.
Some major buildings and some statues defaced. Declaration of endless
war. Parties in the park. Criminalisation of drinking. Several dead
friends. There was experimentation with make-up and electricity.
Occupation of a number of universities. Fist-fights with cops and
fascists. Talks on Russian Futurism in squatted pubs while central
London burned. Distress. Hate speech. Consolidation of royalty.
Running for our lives. It's difficult now — all of that stuff is piled up
like a heap of expressionist rubble in a semi-imaginary alley somewhere
far away. We argue endlessly about whether it was us who died or
them, but the one thing we all agree on is the barbed line that separates
us. Sometimes we pluck that line. It makes a high and barely audible
electric screech, like some useless old record. It puts immense pressure
on the inside of our skulls, like boiling bleach, like the abolition of all
memory. It speaks of heartbreak, of denial, of new advances in
somnambulism. Of revenge fantasies and drug addiction. It has nothing
to say about where to go from here, about the day we crawl out from
under our scattered rocks, and burn their border controls to the ground.
One day our eyes will close. One day the sun will finally go down.

Jane Burn

HOME / HEDGEHOG / AUTISM / COVID HAPPENING TO SOMEONE / SOMEWHERE ELSE?

I told the counsellor that I had been okay,
when she asked how I had been. Good, even.
The roads are so quiet. On my walks, I haven't seen a soul.
I function well in this new confine. *Do autistic people*
feel guilty? I go to the laptop and look myself up,
like (over this last year) I have learned to do.
It's there (I think), buried beneath a few mute layers
like a pea through a mattress. I told the counsellor *I am the happiest*
I have been for a long while. Is this bad? I go to the laptop

and use the statistics to try and make it real. It's real (I think)
and when I read the fear of my Facebook friends, I realise that I am
         unhinged,
am without gravity, am floating away. I smack my palm to my head,
try to thump it in. I feel as if I was built to thrive inside
these new, restricted days. My son cannot go anywhere
and this has taken all the murder / road wreck / violent fears away.
I told the counsellor that I am using predictive text more and more,
to help me show that I care. *I am so sorry. I love you.*
It keeps me looking human, in everyone else's sight.

A hedgehog fell into my neighbour's water bucket during the night,
though we try to be good and catch these precious pools,
try to learn not to squander the gift of useful rain.
The hedgehog sank and it became too much death, much too near.
I thought about the damp skin that closed above its head,
how it saw the dusk through a quivering window,
how it opened its mouth to the shape of the moon.
How the water stole away its tiny breath,
how its spines held a hostage of dew.

I thought about its bed of cold flood, its doused eyes,
its final small and smothering room. It was meant to keep on
crossing the dark road, shadowing the way with its plump wedge,
meant to keep on tramping down its boundaries,
wearing its routes into the eternally familiar. If it can die like this,
then the usual owls might drown in the evening sky,
the bats could fall from the twilight like sad rain —
the trees will end up failing to wear the stars upon their brittle heads.
There will be no more predictability of things.

Ellen van Neerven

LOVE AND TRADITION

for Aunty Nancy Bamaga

rising sea
takes and
breaks into backyards
to trouble families

we cannot live
with the seas in our bellies
we cannot rest
with the sea at our legs

the tide
is coming
to stroke
our dead

we want to know
who unplugged
our island
of childhood

island
of love and tradition
let them see
what has gone under

Owen Sheers

LIABLE TO FLOODS

'Liable to floods' the farmer warned them.
And on the map, the letters arcing down the valley
in black and white
but still the major wouldn't listen —

tipping back his cap with one finger
and laying a fatherly hand on the farmer's shoulder.
'Don't you worry Jack,' he said,
'We've got this one covered.'

And so they made their camp,
a thousand tents across the valley floor,
but even then as the GIs tapped the steel
they felt the backbone of the rock, shallow beneath the soil.

For the next two days they trained
under Moel Siabod's shoulder.
Greenhorns from Kansas, Ohio and Iowa,
sweeping in a line

through the ditches, streams and bracken,
preparing for the landings on Utah and Omaha
pegged as yet to an unknown date
hung somewhere just over the horizon.

On the third night they slept to the sound
of the rain's fusillade and the artillery of thunder,
while outside, under cover of darkness
the river pulled herself up and spread her wings,

bleeding through the camp like ink from a broken cartridge.
The guards were woken by their tin cans and cups
set afloat and clinking against each other
like ghosts in celebration.

They raised the alarm but it was already too late
and the river, arming herself with their rifles,
flushing out the latrines, swallowing the jeeps,
gathered them all and ushered them off.

And as their camp beds became rafts,
gently lifted and spun, more than one GI
woke from dreams of home to sense
just for a second, somewhere deep in the bone,

how suitable this was,
as if the weather had finally caught up with their lives —
this being taken at night without any say,
this being borne, this being swept away.

Rhiannon Hooson

THIRLMERE

After we lit the last candle
the gales couldn't hold us any more.
Along the lane the walls had begun
to slump, water sluicing through them
green as grass, but we drove
through anyway and out into the valley.

The fields were polished flat.
Trees were hung with drooping ropes
of fleece that caught the breeze like kudzu.
Banks of shale sprawled
draining across the roads, and the sky
was open, dizzying and blue, tall into the air
above the crowns of our heads,

and the slate face of the lake
was the same as always. Lakes survive
any flood, lie oblique in their hollows,
streaked with the half-truths of glimpsed reflections.
The birds were only then beginning to sound.
All across the fields the fallen trees were burning.

Gillian Clarke

CANTRE'R GWAELOD

The morning after, the beach at Borth
is a graveyard, a petrified forest
thundered out of the sand by the storm,
drowned by the sea six thousand years ago
when the Earth was flat,
the horizon the edge of the world.

Remains of stilted walkways tell their story:
how she walked over water between trees,
longing for land lost when the sea-god stole it,
fled with her children, shouldered, shawled,
with every creature that could crawl, run, fly,
till time turned truth to myth.

It's how it will be as world turns reflective:
seas sated with meltwater, craving more;
a cliff-fall takes a bungalow; a rising
tide rips up a coastal train-track;
storm fells a thousand-year-old oak,
smashes a graceful seaside promenade.

Grieve for lost wilderness — for the lovesick salmon
lured by sweet river-water sleeved in the salt,
homing upstream to spawn at the source
where it was born; for mating hares
in love with the March wind; for thermals
lifting a flaunt of red kites over the wood;

for bees mooning for honey in weedless fields;
for sleepy Marsh Fritillary butterflies
swarming the ancient bog of Cors Llawr Cwrt;
for the Brown Hairstreak in love with blackthorn
and the honeydew of aphids in the ash;
for the blackbird's evening aria of possession;

for Earth's intricate engineering, unpicked
like the bones, flesh, sinews of the mother duck
crushed on the motorway, her young
bewildered in a blizzard of feathers;
the balance of things undone by money,
the indifferent hunger of the sea.

Vahni Capildeo

THE PETS OF OTHERS

Turtle thrashes opposite the dishwasher,
climbs the water breakline, while the rocks
wait artificially; what sand is needed
being supposable only from flippers
in action, while the chin lifts; she meets the eyes
of tall and dry onlookers. Her red streaks seem
so powerful, a punishable woman's!
Yet compassion flows pointlessly towards her,
like a sable marram dune shifting to make valleys
in which some find rest, from which the sea cannot be glimpsed,
or a way out predicted. Her eggs will come
unfertilized, after how much compulsive
thrashing; and she will be saved from eating them
by her warm-handed keepers, who'd love her wild.

Wendell Berry

THE PEACE OF WILD THINGS

When despair for the world grows in me
and I wake in the night at the least sound
in fear of what my life and my children's lives may be,
I go and lie down where the wood drake
rests in his beauty on the water, and the great heron feeds.
I come into the peace of wild things
who do not tax their lives with forethought
of grief. I come into the presence of still water.
And I feel above me the day-blind stars
waiting with their light. For a time
I rest in the grace of the world, and am free.

George Szirtes

CLIMATE

The sky is broken. There is the usual scud
of dense cloud: showers, lightning, a shower
and then the cycle begins again. Each hour
is a new foray into a thin skim of mud
beside the river. Ducks huddle under leaves
then waddle out into brief sunshine. Nowhere
will you find any fixed point that might bear
your weight or even your spirits. Nothing receives
the imprint of your shoe. It is England of course,
not one of the dependable climates. Things fly
in muscular gusts: flags, bunting, news-sheets.
It is as if there were some irresistible force
blowing us over into a strange new century
that billows beyond us, between our thin heart-beats.

Eavan Boland

HOW WE WERE TRANSFIGURED

Now when darkness starts
in mid-afternoon,
when evening shows an unwelcome
half-sliced winter moon
I remember days
when I never thought twice about
what was farther off
from the four walls of our
house, from the hills
above it, from our infant daughters sleeping
in it or what lay
in wait for us on the Irish Sea
as darkness moved up
and away and we slept late oblivious
to the rain's drizzle,
the tape and flicker of it,
to what was coming
silently, insistently, to render
our lives visible to us again:
light the builder,
light the maker, fitter of roofs to gutters
of the tree's root
to the tree's height,
of earth to sky:
assembler of openings at
the river's mouth and the mind's eye.

Paul Henry

UNDER THE RIVER

Under the river a deeper river runs.
It is simply a case of pressing your ear
your heart to the bank, about here,
then of listening to its quieter turns

to the voices of loved ones
you thought would never rise again,
holding you now, with an old refrain.
Under the river a deeper river runs.

*

Into the dimming light the fish stone,
the flit-spirits, the singing well,
the sudden bleat festival.
And the white manor's sloping lawn

is a tennis court on the run. Rain
salts its lines, makes bull's eyes
of trout kisses. *O... o... O...*
Into the dimming light the fish stone.

*

Some of us are ghosts before we die,
dressing too darkly in summer,
following church bells in winter
down crumbling staircases of sky

to the river, where a deeper river lies
about here. Hush, they are singing well
tonight, as we are singing still
though some of us are ghosts before we die.

Elizabeth-Jane Burnett

LLYN GWYNANT

All through the night I twitch my heart.
Swimming is a kind of hiccup
that jolts the body clean apart.
All through the night I twitch my heart;
tight contractions of sleep starts
break like waves pushing me up.
All through the night I twitch my heart.
Swimming is a kind of hiccup.

And though I wake from something deep,
the pull comes from the darkening lake.
It is not night, I did not sleep.
And though I wake from something deep,
it is not sleep my muscles heap
on bone but waves that gently break.
And though I wake from something deep,
the pull comes from the darkening lake.

Then always afterwards a calm
that flattens out the body's crease,
the water holds me in its palm
and always afterwards a calm,
a wash of mint and lemon balm
and wallflowers (once known as *heart's ease*);
then always afterwards a calm
that flattens out the body's crease.

Vona Groarke

THE RIVERBED

There is sun in the mirror, my head in the trees.
There is sun in the mirror without me.
I am lying face up on the riverbed.
My lover is swimming above me.

The ribbons he tied in my hair are gone,
gone back to their net in the water.
Instead I have silverweed, speedwell and rue,
where once I had his hands to lie on.

Instead I have silverweed, speedwell and rue,
where once I had his arms beneath me.
His body may come as his body has gone —
and the marl will close over again.

Where are your silverweed, your speedwell now?
They have all gone under the water.
Where is your face in the river now?
Drifting upstream to the moon.

I have walked on the floor of the river with you.
I have walked on the floor of the river.
I would lie on the bed of the river with you.
I will lie on the bed of the river.

Jennifer Wong

YANGTZE

Small tourist boats
pass through spectacular relief.

In the valley, you hear a wind
made sublime by the poets.

To weep for what used to be
the largest cradle of fish and shrimps:

the depth of this water's wrath, devouring
the children and stone age relics.

To tame the water dragon
is as impossible as learning to live with it.

Do not ask me where the white dolphins
belong in the bigger river of things;

I don't want to know what happens
to the porpoises. Please stop asking.

Colin Simms

SHE IS IN THE BREAKING OF HER SEAS

She is in the breaking of her seas
on scaur and bar and strand
these flecks flung over Iceland
her plumage; white tips and sand:
her plunge sideslips of command.

Thousands of land-miles and seas
she seized in its abundance in Alaska
prettiest ground-squirrel of the tundra,
bewildering all grand caribou-land
she passes over; a tribute-demand?*

Too easy, the idea of 'enemies'.
Boldness may be best shield against her;
why, then is she "nobler" than skua?
Because she is so much less scavenger,
neither parasite nor pirate. Yet at ease
among categories, free of all law
for no falconer will fully 'mann' her;
little-knowable, rare, rumour, raw.

Alaska 1974

* [based on watching a gyrfalcon 'refuse' the 'alpha' of a group of ground squirrels,
  to return for one evidently injured or ill, after watching them all, as I was doing,
  over half an hour. The 'alpha' animal has made no attempt to escape.]

Mir Mahfuz Ali

MIG-21 RAIDS AT SHEGONTOLA

Only this boy moves
between the runes of trees
on his tricycle
when an eagle swoops,
releases two arrows
from its silver wings and melts
away faster than lightning.
Then a loud whistle
and a bang like dry thunder.
In a blink the boy sees
his house roof sink,
feels his ears ripped off.
The blast puffs up a fawn smoke
bigger than a mountain cloud.
The slow begonias rattle
their scarlet like confetti.
Metal slashes
the trees and ricochets.
Wires and pipes snap
at the roots, quiver.
The whirling smoke packed
with bricks and cement,
chicken feathers and nigella seeds.
When the cloud begins
to settle on the ground,
the boy makes out buckled iron rods.
White soot descends
and he finds himself dressed
like an apprentice baker.

Fiona Benson

EUROFIGHTER TYPHOON

My daughters are playing outside with plastic hoops;
the elder is trying to hula, over and over —
it falls off her hips, but she keeps trying,
and the younger is watching and giggling,
and they're happy in the bright afternoon.
I'm indoors at the hob with the door open
so I can see them, because the elder might trip,
and the younger is still a baby and liable to eat dirt,
when out of clear skies a jet comes in low
over the village. At the first muted roar
the elder runs in squealing then stops in the kitchen,
her eyes adjusting to the dimness, looking foolish
and unsure. I drop the spoon and bag of peas
and leave her frightened and tittering, wiping my hands
on my jeans, trying to walk and not run,
because I don't want to scare the baby
who's still sat on the patio alone, looking for her sister,
bewildered, trying to figure why she's gone —
all this in the odd, dead pause of the lag —
then sound catches up with the plane
and now its grey belly's right over our house
with a metallic, grinding scream
like the sky's being chainsawed open
and the baby's face drops to a square of pure fear,
she tips forward and flattens her body on the ground
and presses her face into the concrete slab.
I scoop her up and she presses in shuddering,
screaming her strange, *halt* pain cry
and it's all right now I tell her again and again,
but it's never all right now — Christ have mercy —
my daughter in my arms can't steady me —
always some woman is running to catch up her children,
we dig them out of the rubble in parts like plaster dolls —
Mary Mother of God have mercy, mercy on us all.

Ross Cogan

RAGNARÖK

After Milosz

When it comes, and it will, it will come on
a plain weekday, perhaps in early spring
or autumn, a frowsy day, one that woke late
and got dressed in a hurry without care
quite forgetting
to comb its hair, which anyway got damp

in the almost rain. When it comes the slugs
will have been on the lettuces again,
chiselling their sickle moons; starlings will sit
like notes on a stave while below them men spray
hectares of grain
with a lake of liquid manure. A snake

will riffle its green belt through the fern stems
and the flies will alight on a dead shrew.
When it comes a young woman will be
formatting the numbers in her spreadsheet
as she scrolls through
a list of annual reports. The bond

salesman will have made the biggest trade
of his career; sparrows will jive outside
in the puddles; fungi will start to fling
armfuls of spores into the air; a spent
rabbit will hide
shaking from the hounds. And when it comes

the man in the fourteenth-floor flat, the one
the other tenants never see, will pop
a pill and think again of his dead child.
The women walking in the park behind
their prams will stop
to hear the song unfurl through the window.

The slaughtermen will have stained their gloves red
with slick, bright blood; tectonic plates will move
under the sea a fraction of an inch
and cause no harm; a poet will write sadly
of his lost love
and pick his nose. The President will put

the final touches to the plan for peace.
Don't be surprised then if you fail to spot
the golden ranks of heroes or the massed
brigades of ogres. These days they wear grey
and look a lot
like each other. But they remain heroes

and ogres, and their swords gleam in their bags.
A one-eyed man will pull on his broad-brimmed hat
and stalk away. Please don't expect a warning.
This is a whimper not a bang, but it's
a whimper that
will level hills and drown the suffering world.

Rebecca Tamás

WITCH WOOD

the witch thinks about what it would be like to
fuck woods and not the government
the stretch of land is green but has redness in the soil
the trees gather around a path from Roman times which
has sunk into the ground an opening flashing and brightening
fucking the trees is giving back the means of production to the trees
xylem and blood vessel outreach tell me how it is when there's a storm
not that different because we all shake but some don't
have a shelter it can't be made romantic branches are entering
different parts of your body
is that right different parts of your body are entering
branches you are shouting loudly and thistles racketing about in
here inside your radical opening and singular throat sounds
for this to work you can't spend more than four hours on the ground
clearing bracken or cutting
because it ruins so easily when it is not a choice the tree is taking

water from you drenching and it has an archive of season
and this is what it is like to feel snow pushing hard in between your legs
cold and magisterial and probably not in any widely available porno
when the summer gets in there inside the pockets of your arms
open sweaty mouth space is being made
that widens and separates more and more and
you look the same but really green hair
you forget the words for assessment criteria for investigation
for intersection for fence for phallus for trunk for
the thing the thing the thing
one solar panel opening eat it up and eat it up
stacked cream layers of light skin just touching the next fine membrane of
        skin
the page with a hoof mark a peaking stain

Kei Miller

TO KNOW GREEN FROM GREEN

'And all this in a million shades of green.'
— James Henderon, describing Jamaica

To know the nearby bushes you must know green from green
know seafoam different from sea, teal different from tea,
& still a million shades between.

Must know hunter different from army different from rifle,
a shot fired causes birds to lift, screaming from the trees,
that 'screamin' is itself a shade of green.

Look: a parakeet, its wings bright against the night,
you must know midnight different from malachite different
from the leathery shade called crocodile.

You must know emerald different from jade; know greens that travel
towards grey — laurel, artichoke, sage. Forest is different from jungle
is different from tree which is itself a shade of green.

You must know India, Paris & Pakistan, that breeze
can rustle language out of leaves: Spanish, Persian, Russian,
& still a million tongues between.

Medbh McGuckian

THE COLONY ROOM

If you are touching, you are also being touched:
if I place my hands in prayer, palm to palm,
I give your hands new meaning, your left hand calm.

You define my body with the centre of your hand;
I hear through the shingled roof of your skin
your ear-shaped body enter the curved floor-line
of my skin. My hands just skim the cushioned opening,
the glitter of your mouth; all woods, roots and flowers
scent and stretch the map that covers your body.

Less touchable than the birth or continuation
of Ireland, in its railed enclosure, your root-note,
in its sexual climate, your kingdom-come eyes,
year-long, inactive lover, durable as paradise.

Like small shocks in the winter, neck to neck,
the mirrors reflected the coloured ray
the evenings needed most, when the day…
asked for night in that mistletoe way.

Richard Gwyn

TAKING ROOT

'A rootless individual who takes root
wherever he finds himself'

He knows he cannot belong,
that he will always be a foreigner;
nor ever will be a true Levantine,
unless he puts down roots: a paradox.
So, he settles for a while
— he cannot think in terms of
a permanent arrangement — in Beirut,
meets a nice Christian girl,
who bears him five children in ten years,
all of them fine and strong,
and he enjoys the easy yoke (or so he sees it)
of work and marriage. With the stolen silver
from the blind man of Tarsus
he opens an emporium of herbs and spices,
which soon becomes a small empire
with shops in the Lebanon, Alexandria,
Saloniki, Istanbul. The Levant is his oyster,
and he builds the family home in Smyrna:
here there are fewer constraints on
his pursuits (libidinal and fiscal)
and he can direct operations from
a seat of privilege. He blasts several enemies
to make way for his growing enterprise;
charters camel trains; forms a private army,
bribing brigands into service
to ensure that traders

through the Caucasus pay his levies.
He breaks into dried fruit; dates, figs,
raisins, for the European market,
monitors the opium trade, and
commands a monopoly in time for
the morphine boom of World War One.
But he knows that on the horizon
hovers a terrible conclusion
to all that he's contrived to build.

* Definition of a Levantine, attributed to Georges Zananiri Pasha (supposedly the model for Balthazar in Lawrence Durrell's *Alexandria Quartet*) cited from Zananiri's memoir *Entre mer et désert* (1996) in Philip Mansell's *Levant* (2010: p.269).

John Kinsella

PENILLION OF CORMORANTS IN POLLUTED RIVER

Wings out to dry

Those snake-necked birds
Perch on absurd
Protrusions, test
Pillar and post

Eyeing *below,*
Plan and follow
Their beaks deep down
Past light, then crown

Metal surface,
As shadow splits
Like mercury —
As mercury:

Wings out to dry

Ailing fish skive
Making each dive
Easier . . . then
Fruitless — those thin

Skins so rattled,
Their contents dead
Before being
Killed off: seeing

Their own dead-ends
As whose Godsend?
Bright red speedboats
Would have us gloat.

Wings out to dry

And nesting trees,
Dead colonies:
So few are left
Here, blue eggs lost.

Who feeds baited
Fishhooks to pied
Cormorants, fish
Still in distress?

They stare further
Than disaster,
Their bald raven
Revolution.

Wings out to dry

Leo Boix

GOLDFINCH COMES TO TELL US THERE'S A FIRE AT THE END OF OUR GARDEN, HE

lands
on my hand,
    carries bad news, a fire broke out
    in our courtyard, puffs out
       his bronze chest, then begins his report;

There
where the chair
    is, something bursting sparks, he's surprised
    how fast flames grow in size,
       how thunderous they are. He can't believe

it,
not one bit.
    He explains, his black and yellow wings
    fluttering fast: Charred string,
       scorched twigs, half-burnt feathers and a corpse.

His
high-pitch whizz
    picks up speed, he cannot stop. Crackling
    sounds grow louder, flashing
       flames on our plane tree. Fire surrounds us.

The
house, bins, the
    ivy climbed by dark orange glares, sky
    turns ominous, ash flies,
        and there, at the end of our garden

tall
the giant ball
    glows a bright red, maroon, resplendent,
    blowing shards, magenta.
        It takes us a lifetime to see it.

Sheenagh Pugh

VISITOR

Sometimes, after a storm, sand shifts,
stones are flung aside, and a skull
stares out, or a framework of ribs
startles with its whiteness. Whole villages
have come back: hearths, stone tables,
even the shelves built into their walls.

Captured then, before they could resume
the skin they left on the rocks, they live
in our light, all their arrangements,
oil lamps, loom weights, open, like a bombed house,
its front wall gone, forced to display
carpets and wallpapers to public view.

The one nearby, though, was more slippery.
A layer of rock slid away from a shape
two thousand years old; it was photographed,
but the cliff lurched again and took back
this brief acquaintance, the neighbour who called in
just once, and whom we never got to know.

Gerry Loose

AFTER AMERGIN

am glacier rolling back
am tsunami
am beaching whale
am the bones of every curlew
am stag starving on hill
am hawk down to bone
am wilt of green plant
am ribcage hind
am salmon infested with lice
am the end of words
am burning teardrop
am salt ocean in woodland
am plastic in every pore
am head burst with fire

who gouges & grubs blue mountains
who trudges the crescent moon
who stores suns in buried bunkers
who leaches the fecund topsoils
whose alibi is god
who stands at the edge
who holds back the typhoon

Cath Drake

HOW I HOLD THE WORLD IN THIS CLIMATE EMERGENCY

Sometimes I hold world in one hand, my life
in the other and I get cricks in my neck
as the balance keeps swinging. I walk uneasily.

Sometimes I am bent over with the sheer weight of world,
eyes downcast, picking up useful things from the ground.

Sometimes one shoulder is pulling toward an ear
as if it's trying to block the ear from hearing but can't reach.

Sometimes my body is a crash mat for world. I want to say
'I'm sorry I'm sorry!' but don't say it aloud.
I am privileged so I should be able to do something.

Sometimes I lie on my side and grasp world like a cushion.
I'm soft and young, and don't feel I can change anything.
I nudge world with affection, whispering: I know, I know.

Sometimes I build a cubby from blankets thrown across furniture.
There is only inside, no outside. When I was a child,
world was a small dome and change came summer by summer.

Sometimes I make a simple frame with my arms to look at world.
I'm not involved directly. It carries on without me.
This way I can still love the sky, its patterns of clouds and contrails.

Sometimes I'm chasing world through the woods, bursting
with hope and adrenalin. Oh God, am I running!
I want to keep moving. My mouth is full of fire.

Some days are like bread and milk. I just get on with pouring
and buttering. I want the little things to be what matters most again.

Sometimes I hold little: I'm limp and ill.
Days barely exist. It's enough to make soup.

Penelope Shuttle

'THE WORLD HAS PASSED' [1]

On the other side of the rose
there is the felling of trees

On the other side of the frost
there is the colour of a bruise

On the other side of the ovum
there is the woman of warfare

On the other side of the bonfire
there is the music springing back,
the retaliation

On the other side of the leaf
is the lesson in leafmaking

On the other side of the room
is a cabinet of curiosities, antique granary

On the other side of the mother
is a sigh full of filaments,
a few words walking on tiptoe

On the other side of the blackberry
is the harvest of the moon

[1] Yokut term for 'a year has gone by'.

On the other side of the voice
is the absence of the waterfall

On the other side of the ice
is the half-satisfied sea

On the other side of the blood
is the unrooted child

On the other side of the child
is the gulping-down of cloud,

the whispering of loopholes—
arrival at the fresh shrine

David Baker

PASTORAL

Here at the center	of a field	of green
leaves waving	center of a	grief I can't
see far enough	to tell how	it will ease
it will not ease	it goes on	and on now
as yours does	in sunlight	and in rain
holding hands with	her in the	last minutes
sky so vast	hear the	wheat roar —

Seán Hewitt

MEADOW

The lane stitched with hazel,
and by the gate the elderflower,
lifted, its fifty constellations
splitting open on the branch.

Because I didn't know it then,
I walked out from the house
into the warm field, took
the sun on my face, passed

the beehive's sultry
murmur. In the lime-shadows,
I watched each floret and petal
inscribe life in its colour.

I found a bone — broken;
saw the cormorant dip
beneath the water — lost it
before it rose. And, because

you died the next day, before
I could instil every image
of your life, I commit all this
to memory: the ox-eyes

and the mallow-flower,
the sea of barley moving;
the cornflower, and the spark
of the snapweed; the light-

emerald I photographed
where I saw it — stilled against
the soil — and brought home
to your bed to show you.

Paula Meehan

DEATH OF A FIELD

The field itself is lost the morning it becomes a site
When the Notice goes up: Fingal County Council — 44 units

The memory of the field is lost with the loss of its herbs

Though the woodpigeons in the willow
The finches in what's left of the hawthorn hedge
And the wagtail in the elder
Sing on their hungry summer song

The magpies sound like flying castanets

And the memory of the field disappears with its flora:
Who can know the yearning of yarrow
Or the plight of the scarlet pimpernel
Whose true colour is orange?

The end of the field is the end of the hidey holes
Where first smokes, first tokes, first gropes
Were had to the scentless mayweed

The end of the field as we know it is the start of the estate
The site to be planted with houses each two- or three-bedroom
Nest of sorrow and chemical, cargo of joy

The end of dandelion is the start of Flash
The end of dock is the start of Pledge
The end of teazel is the start of Ariel
The end of primrose is the start of Brillo
The end of thistle is the start of Bounce
The end of sloe is the start of Oxyaction
The end of herb robert is the start of Brasso
The end of eyebright is the start of Persil

Who amongst us is able to number the end of grasses
To number the losses of each seeding head?

                                    I'll walk out once
Barefoot under the moon to know the field
Through the soles of my feet to hear
The myriad leaf lives green and singing
The million million cycles of being in wing

That — before the field become map memory
In some archive on some architect's screen
I might possess it or it possess me
Through its night dew, its moon-white caul
Its slick and shine and its profligacy
In every wingbeat in every beat of time

Carol Rumens

EASTER SNOW

"There was a man of double deed
Sowed his garden full of seed . . ."
Anon

"And so I've found my native country . . ."
Attila Jozsef

There was a man of double deed
Sowed his garden full of snow,
Lit a stove he could not feed,
Sired a child he could not grow.
Who fashioned birds from wooden blocks,
And when their wings fused flight to dark,
And when the dark swept through the locks,
Fetched a book and made an ark.
But who could sail so deep a ship,
Or marry beast to bolting beast,
Dance as he would his flimsy whip
Over the backs of the deceased?

Poets must tell the truth, you said:
The poor must, too, although they lie.
We listen at your iron bed,
Under the tunnel of the sky,
And ask you softly what you need —
Blue roller skates? A football team?
But you are far and far indeed.
And all the stumbling magi bring
Is the smoke-haze of a dream,
A floating girl, a greasy bear,
A courtyard echo-echoing
The snow wing-beats of your heart
Towards the deficit of air
Predicted in your natal chart.

Rachael Boast

AGRARIAN SONG

Mars was once considered a god of the soil,
which seems about right, given the effort
of turning it. I sang as I worked;
I sang for you; I sang to let the muscles
of my back know *this could go on all day.*

I pulled at horsetail. The hurt earth's
claim on it seemed intricate.
Its effort is the effort of resistance —
each root-node, palpably unclasped,
made for a tug-of-war with the unseen.

The effort of the earthworm contorts
his volume headlong.
Drawing the missing half of his world
down like a hood, he'd have seen stars,
pushing like that, into the pixels of his darkness.

You're taken with this muck under my nails,
these gardener's hands that crackle
along your arms like flame. Plant in me
the effort of your dark songs.
Constellate them.

Deryn Rees-Jones

NIGHTJAR

Listen to the nightjar, hear her holy tremblings —
star litter, night fragment, slip down a spine of grass.
A circumstance of sound electrifies the heath,
opens up the dark. Though she's dead now,
or to all effects, in silence, gone
like a ghost ship rising, you can hear her.
Her voice is both inside you
and around you. She pushes you away,
she asks you to be near.
In the stillness, let the sound debris, in wild track,
moth-like, poke the dust. Put your finger on the space
she finds in you, her rattle notes, her love rambles:
let her open up a space, beside you — there
now, there — close beside your heart.

Vievee Francis

NIGHTJAR

Its flight was soundless, the wings full of air.
The feathers. The feathers. I didn't imagine this.
I opened my eyes and there above me it hovered,
as if considering what should happen next.
I was not yet asleep. It was dusk. But I had worked
since dawn and needed to rest. Let myself collapse
upon the bed. Had I opened a window?
It seemed to float. I could feel the rapidity
of its heart. It stared as if it did not know it was staring.
Not wanting to frighten it I did not reach, though
I wanted to. It remained just inches away. Reluctant incubus.
Crepuscular darling. How could I fear it? So urgent—
my muscles relaxed as I concentrated
all of my attention on the intruder—so hesitant.
I mouthed, *Lower*. I lay still as an invitation.

Aimee Nezhukumatathil

INVITATION

Come in, come in. The water's fine! You can't get lost
here. Even if you want to hide behind a clutch
    of spiny oysters—I'll find you. If you ever leave me
    at night, by boat, you'll see the arrangement

of red-gold sun stars in a sea of milk. And though
it's tempting to visit them—stay. I've been trained
    to gaze up all my life, no matter the rumble
    on earth, but I learned it's okay to glance down

into the sea. So many lessons bubble up if you know
where to look. Clouds of plankton churning
    in open whale mouths might send you east
    and chewy urchins will slide you west. Squid know

how to be rich when you have ten empty arms.
Can you believe there are humans who don't value
    the feel of a good bite and embrace at least once a day?
    Underneath you, narwhals spin upside down

while their singular tooth needles you
like a compass pointed towards home. If you dive
    deep enough where imperial volutes and hatchetfish
    swim, you will find all the colors humans have not yet

named, and wide caves of black coral and clamshell.
A giant squid finally let itself be captured
    in a photograph, and the paper nautilus ripple-flashes
    scarlet and two kinds of violet when it silvers you near.

Who knows what will happen next? And if you still want
to look up, I hope you see the dark sky as oceanic—
    boundless, limitless—like all the shades of blue in a glacier.
    Listen how this planet spins with so much fin, wing, and fur.

Em Strang

WATER OF AE

Don't wait to walk out along the back-roads
to the boggy fields where the swans are.
You can cross the river at the small bridge
and walk a walk you've walked for ten years
every day, even when the rain's on hard
and the wind's tearing at you. Don't wait
thinking you've seen it all already —
the flooded fields, the brown river,
the white swans. You can't see these things
from the bog-eye of a human. Don't wait.
Stride out with your boots on or, better still,
barefoot, and be inside the wind a while,
be inside the field like a grass halm might,
like a single blade awaiting sunlight.
Don't wait. Inevitably, it takes time
to unzip your hair, your skin, your face
enough to see swans, their blazing white,
but don't wait thinking you need better boots
or a waterproof that'll keep out the rain.
It won't. Don't wait. Walk out entirely
as though the mind is a rook's nest
in a tall, far-off Scots pine and behold
for the first time the swans, still there
after ten years of your looking, hunched
in the Scottish weather.
It doesn't matter how many similes
climb down from the rook's nest —
none of them fit. Don't wait.

Bob Hicok

LUSH

Trees talk to each other,
the book on my kitchen table
told me before I went to bed last night,
through roots that braid and scents
emitted to warn of predators.
They even seem to make friends,
encroaching less upon the canopy
of a bud, for whom they'll bring back
a curry if they run down to the shop.
Old trees, anyway. Commercial forests
aren't around long enough
for this intimacy to evolve, so your Christmas tree's
definitely a loner and your Chanukah tree's
an interesting melding of two faiths,
good on you, you hybrid m.f. I'm looking

at a scrap of fog a quarter mile off
and wondering
if I touch a cedar here,
will a cedar there feel my affection
at the rate
of three inches per second,
or if I bite it, if I tell it
I'm lonely for what it has
though swaddled
by learning yet again
where intelligence hides, how thoughts flow
through air and ground
in a way I can't invent, only destroy. I don't know

how I'll ever prune a tree again
or give up on the whisper *God*
to suggest the engine of thoughtfulness
that surrounds us, the wombing fluency of matter
to matter in its mutations
to itself, to connect
form to form and listen
and rile and roar. Swaddled, embraced,
absorbed: I live inside the dream
of a mind that goes as far
as going goes, call life
homunculus, call all distances
closed, call touching and fondness
what they are: *roads home*.

Jennifer Hunt

SEPTEMBER

This evening
picking beans after a thunder shower
shed blossoms cling like drab insects
to my fingers.
Late sun, yellow as pumpkin flowers.

Now, with my colander,
by the open kitchen door,
the sun makes a square on the red lino.
Outside, white hens peck at shreds of light.

Soon bats will draw down the dark,
but I'll leave the door open,
breathe in the honeysuckle air
while moths circle the lampshade
dizzy from touching the moon.

Simon Armitage

I KICKED A MUSHROOM

and then I felt bad.
And not just some cute toadstool or gnome's bed
but a fruiting body of brain-coloured disks
as wide as a manhole cover or bin lid,
a raft of silky caps basted in light rain
stemming from one root as thick as a wrist,
anchored in deep earth, like a rope on a beach.
One jab with a spade would have done the job,
then a pitchfork to hoik it over the hedge,
but I stuck in the boot then walked away
with its white meat caught in my tongue and lace.
All night it lies on the lawn inside out,
its tripes and corals turned to the stars,
gills in the air, showing the gods what I am.

Jane Hirshfield

IN A KITCHEN WHERE MUSHROOMS WERE WASHED

In a kitchen where mushrooms were washed,
the mushroom scent lingers.

As the sea must keep for a long time the scent of the whale.

As a person who's once loved completely,
a country once conquered,
does not release that stunned knowledge.

They must want to be found, those strange-shaped, rising morels,
clownish puffballs.

Lichens have served as a lamp-wick.
Clean-burning coconuts, olives.
Dried salmon, sheep fat, a carcass of petrel set blazing:
light that is fume and abradement.

Unburnable mushrooms are other.
They darken the air they come into.

Theirs the scent of having been traveled, been taken.

Sina Queyras

FROM 'ENDLESS INTER-STATES': 1

They go down to the expressways, baskets
In hand, they go down with rakes, shovels
And watering cans, they go down to pick

Beans and trim tomato plants, they go down
In wide-brimmed hats and boots, passing
By the glass-pickers, the Geiger counters, those

Guarding the toxic wastes. They go down
Remembering the glide of automobiles, the
Swelter of children in back seats, pinching, twitching,

Sand in their bathing suits, two-fours of Molson's
In the trunk of the car. They go down, past
The sifters, the tunnellers, those who transport

Soil from deep in the earth, and are content
To have the day before them, are content to imagine
Futures they will inhabit, beautiful futures

Filled with unimagined species, new varieties of
Plant life, sustainable abundance,
An idea of sufficient that is global. Or,

Because cars now move on rails underground,
The elevated roads are covered in earth,
Vines drape around belts of green, snake

Through cities, overgrown and teeming
With grackles and rats' nests, a wall
Of our own devising, and the night

Watchmen with their machine guns
Keeping humans, the intoxicated,
Out. I am sorry for this version, offer

You coffee, hot while there is still
Coffee this far north, while there is still news
To wake up to, and seasons

Vaguely reminiscent of seasons.

Jennifer Militello

THERE REMAIN NEW BRANCHES

I can imagine such a place: like a flute, it comes apart.
Streets loosen like tobacco. There are animal skins.

It comes across, the way bodies' crying reaches us
and crawls inside. It is beyond the mirrored room

of my sister's eye. It has such a dark iris no light
comes through, and the shed light of rain becomes

a neutral sound. Here we remember what it's like
to remember. Naming parts of the body, we find

they are familiar. Dreams never make the transfer
to days, and the gladioli are wilting.

Welcome to changing everything. Welcome to starving
out of sleep. By morning, weariness will have replaced

the jawbones of a thinned and willful sky.
This illness is savage. These clouds, they are scythes.

Will Stone

THE EXTINCTION PLAN

Moments of pain, progress driven,
the unwelcome clarity of time's incision
enhanced by the new drug day,
where late crimes roll and bask
and suddenly woken eyes, lepers
peer in on hastening apocalypse.

The drone of no return, the settling
of old scores, of charcoal petals,
the cinder path of all that is predicted.
She who never arrived one step ahead
and all around you the embalmed
the catacombed, erect in their niches.

The extinction plan in motion,
as cut price flights steeply climb,
over Ensor's cornered skeleton.

In order to go on Schubert pens,
Munch paints *Death and the Maiden*.
Strindberg runs through the Latin Quarter
brandishing his hands, black and burned
from experiments with sulphur.

Each repeats what has gone before.
The earth can take another sack of fear,
a single life's strict toiling,
embittered aging, the dead weight of loss,
a case of cherished photographs
and a few last sprigs of joy.

No one wants to be dust.
No one wants their love left out,
but nearly every wheel finds the rail
and follows the tramline to lust.

In one dive billions of krill find God.
Ghostly, like a low gas flame
they go on a while unseen, they exist
to explain the blue whale's darkness.

Peter Sirr

WHALEFALL

Every so often a windfall whale will blow through the depths
and where it lodges the pitchblack waters begin to stir,
specialists in their brilliant bodies to wake and move

towards their reward: a slow devouring, months of it,
the hagfish and rat-tails, crabs and sleeper sharks
picking the carcass clean until the bones collapse

but now the bone-world begins: *osedax*, the bone-eating worms
with their feathery plumes, blown like bubbles from the last whalefall
lock on and feed, generation after generation

until the place is empty again, a sulphide nothingness
the eggs have already fled, riding the currents for the fall
where it all goes on, the endlessly resisting life, the whale pulse.

Katrina Naomi

THE BEACH COULDN'T BE FOUND

under the scorched weed and rubbish, the crows,
the human shit they fed on. The water was so far out,

nothing you'd swim in. Only the dogs sunbathed,
their fleas popping in the heat like corn.

The sea was no colour and there was no path
through the broken things, flies wafting up

and resettling. There could be no way through for us.
The beach didn't know it was a beach,

didn't know what was expected, that it had duties
to perform. No one had told it and it hadn't asked.

The beach was just a place where the land finished.
We were as welcome and as unwelcome as anyone.

Rhian Edwards

THE GULLS ARE MUGGING

The gulls are mugging the scholars again;
stalking lunches on parade, making nests
of hapless human scalps. It is then they unhinge
the jaws, snatch the booty whole, broad daylight
poaching from your unwelcoming hand.

Don't let the dove feathers fool you,
the slapstick march or the witless China
doll eyes. They could shawl all their plumage
around you in a burlesque stole, smokescreen
you away into the perfect vanishing act.

They can dip bread in the ocean, bait fish
into their tricking beaks. They have no qualms
pecking chunks from a whale hide when it surfaces
to breathe. They mate for life to rival the romance
of the swan, taking turns to brood until the chicks fledge.

Far from birdbrained, this is organized crime;
these rogue pickpocketers, mob raiders, white suited
butchers. And they have all the elements covered:
these camp criers of the skies, fishwives of the seas,
unpacified foul mouths of this concrete square.

Samuel Tongue

FISH COUNTER

Fish that have a pebble in their heads; Fish that hide in winter;
Fish that feel the influence of stars; Extraordinary prices paid for
certain fish.

> Pliny. *The Natural History*

Cod that have been skinned. Cod that have a pebble
of dill butter in their heads. Cod breaded. Cod battered:
tempura or traditional. Smoked haddock. Dyed haddock.
Wise lumps of raw tuna. Scaled, pin-boned pollock, de-scented:
There are olfactory limits. Bake in the bag; no mess.
"This piece of halibut is good enough for Jehovah".
Fishsticks pink as lads' mags. Skirts and wet fillets
of sole. Fish fingers mashed from fragments of once-fish.
Hake three-ways. *Extraordinary prices paid for certain fish.*
Monkfish defrocked, gurnards gurning, fish so ugly
you must eat them blindfold. Choose before the ice melts.

Philip Gross

THE FLOES

The floes are breaking up now. Some nights,

thinking back, she sees a blue-black slightly
glowing hull: that year, another, and the space

between them like dark sky beneath the surface
heaving, clouding when foam flushes over

while on some chilly fragment, as if sat for ever
on the naughty step, or in her impenetrable

own game, the child of her waits; and will
wait for as long as it takes, until the dark gap

between it all narrows again, something stops
this sliding apart of the galaxies, the starlight

thinning, floes like further houses, their late
windows switched out one by one, once recognized

names like bird cries heard from far off, over ice.

Alice Oswald

SEABIRD'S BLESSING

We are crowds of seabirds,
makers of many angles,
workers that unpick a web
of the air's threads and tangles.

Pray for us when we fight
the wind one to one;
let not that shuddering strength
smash the cross of the wing-bone.

O God the featherer,
lift us if we fall;
preserve the frenzy in our mouths,
the yellow star in the eyeball.

Christ, make smooth the way
of a creature like a spirit
up from its perverse body
without weight or limit.

Holy ghost of heaven,
blow us clear of the world,
give us the utmost of the air
to heave on and to hold.

Pray for us this weird
bare place — we are screaming
O sky count us not as nothing
O sea count us not as nothing

Abeer Ameer

THE STORYTELLER

Aesop had nothing on her. The children gather
on the rooftop level with the heads of Najaf's palm trees,
sit cross-legged ready for stories before bed.
An uneasy weight on her chest; she'd found her youngest
trapping sparrows again.

> *There was and how much there was...*
> She tells the story of a beautiful bulbul.
> Shiny feathers, bright plumes,
> how its song filled the air
> until the king ordered it be caught
> and caged, kept for his eyes only.
> Soon its feathers greyed,
> the light in its eyes vanished,
> the song in its throat withered.

Her eyes wander to that space,
empty since his fourth birthday.
She continues:

> The bulbul's mournful mother
> searched everywhere for her child,
> unable to eat or sleep.
> Both died from sadness.
> The king, filled with remorse,
> promised to protect all his kingdom's
> wildlife. Then he became the kindest,
> wisest king on earth.
> > *And they lived a happy life.*

She looks to the stars, mutters
When you cling to a thing you love it dies.
Sometimes when you love you must let go...must let go.
Her soft voice trails off. The children focus on the cigarette
in her left hand which balances a tower of ash.
In her right hand, amber prayer beads:
her thumb strokes the top of each before moving it along.
She recites *Al-Fatiha*, scans the sky for the crescent moon.

Sam Wilson Fletcher

DARK ECOLOGY

Gently in your fingers   like an egg   hold me to the light
like a hand holding a bulb   am I full of bones?   Are there
black branches   silhouetted veins   Hold me to your ear
do you hear   not the sea   A baritone warmth   A running bath
its slap and splash   stripped of sharpness   Half submerged
buried in scotchegg layers   a red baby   coiled   listening
With your tonguetip   taste me   Do I smell   sunwarm
of hair at temple or nape   Am I faintly musty   do you
detect genitals?   Hold me gently   against the night
do you see glowworms   the depth of trees   are bumblebees
crouched in hollows   does a pelican swoop   is it frightening?
Peer in   through windows foggy with breath   A table
set for dinner   a foaming bathtub   Holding me gently
in your fingers   like an egg   tap me on an edge of stone
or wood   to crack a smile   knock in a few teeth   set your
thumbtips   and hinge me open   What flows out   is it blood

Mimi Khalvati

EGGS

From the first egg I ever drew, brown, speckled,
and pasted on a screen in kindergarden,
through all the eggs I ever ate, fried, scrambled,
boiled, poached, etc., down to this broken

yolk on a plate under my nose, my love
of eggs, in any shape or form, has grown.
Take the form: the prolate symmetry of
a spheroid, weightless when an egg is blown;

the air sac that expands with age and grades
an egg or backlights when you candle it
a blood red embryo; the sun-yolk shades

from marigolds the hens were fed at dawn;
the albumen: water out of which spirit
and embodiment, double-yoked, are drawn.

Jane Lovell

EXHIBIT, 'SONG OF LOST SPECIES'

(O N C A, Brighton, 2016)

Bell jar, in a row of bell jars
holding only silence
and a memory of birdsong:

thin wisps of birds, half-remembered
dreams of birds, airborne waifs
pared from wind and reeds

balanced on tines of wire
in gallery light,
their calls the grief of dwindling.

This one labelled Bewick's wren,
others names we do not recognise.

With their final breath they sing to us:

*'Scoop me up, my bones lighter
than stalks, feathers that fracture
in your fingers; remember.'*

On the screen, we see forests
of birds, trees teeming with life,
peep and shriek and trill.

We take home a flutter of wings,
the thinnest piping,
a future emerging from banks of mist.

We tell our children: *'Watch this.
Remember…'*

Helen Bowell

BARMAN IN EDEN

In the autumn, the barman and I visit Eden.
They have put up signs since the last time I was here.

Some say: DO NOT WALK ON THE GRASS;
others inform guests about the mass extinction.

A dragonfly bumps into a leaf. A peregrine
falcon nose-dives. A mother asks us for money.

I want to change everything
and nothing. The barman takes my hand,

suggests a tea break. I buy a fresh scone.
It is the exact shape of the barman's fist.

In the gift shop, we touch everything:
HOPE is printed in big letters on tea towels.

I know time is measured in Celsius.
At least I have enjoyed the seasons.

When we go home, even the sun
looks away.

Martha Sprackland

GONE INTO THE GARDEN

She stared idly, late afternoon, just picking up
the few degraded plastic bags from the gravel path
and stuffing them into the bin by the back door,
then went inside to make a cup of tea, perhaps
get on with a little work or start dinner.
But at the window, waiting for the kettle's click,
she spotted blue plastic string flapping gently
from the apex of the buddleia. And once she'd gone
back out and fetched it down she found a little hoard
of blackened foil, and balled that up.
And tugged some faded labels from their beds,
and snapped the overreaching twigs, and unburied
a useful length of dirty clothesline and wound it into reels.
And here she paused, and saw much more to do,
and moved deeper into the garden, which grew
and changed around her. She trod down weeds,
pulled her jumper down over her hands
and pushed aside the coiling thorns.
Sometime much later, emptying the standing water
from a rusted pail, scraping dead leaves into piles,
she came across the backless mirror leaning by a tree
with its studs of fossilising snails, its clouded throw.
Back, way back, from the square of the kitchen window
the new husband watched his new wife
digging like a murderer in the darkness.

Duncan Bush

COUCH GRASS

Slow green fire,
shaggy pelt
of the plot's neglect,

each shock-haired
tussock levered loose
with the fork-prongs

rough-edged
enough to crisscross
your palms with cuts.

Gloved you straighten
shaking soil,
Perseus brandishing

the Medusa head
like a trophy scalp.
Tossed, it hisses

in the bonfire's yellow
smoke. Underground
it's already rife

as new rumour in deltas
of knotted fibres,
coarse white jointed net

that will spread
choking
the earth

if not the Earth
aswing
in its old string bag of meridians.

Tamar Yoseloff

KNOTWEED

Durable, your rough roots, your troops;
your line of destruction

that moles its way beneath foundations —
it will outlive us.

We are coming and going, always lost and losing,
in love with the tug of leaving, the future

cast upon the shaded map, the Alice Universe
expanding:

all roads are chosen, all roads say *come*;
your greedy paws claw all for one

to feed your lust for land,
you grab the lot.

Fleeceflower, the fleet hour of inflorescence
bursts, you drape your skirts

over the earth, tough peduncle,
homunculus. You will not budge

now you've found your calling: the felling
of our failing structures.

Siobhán Campbell

THE LONGING OF THE BEES

Gather together, whisper into the ferns, send a trill
out with the mistle thrush. What we have to learn
is that they must be heard. If they arrive all at once
to remind us of a plague, mutant in their anger,
loud in their sway, then we might be persuaded,
even while netting drains, sealing the gaps in outer doors.

Be ready to puncture that inner ear, it is no longer
needed. Brace yourself for commotion. A brouhaha
if ever you saw one. Tumult of absence, uproar of lack.
Without them it seems, nothing is fertile; wheat becomes
an illusion, oil will not press from seeds that were not crossed.

Who knew the workers had a feel for dork and drone?
Castrati singing in our ears while we sweltered,
checking our influence in waves of disproportion.
Research shows that genes are not the problem.
We resolve to put a capsule into space, a narrative
for those who may yet come. Listen to the hedges
it will say. Remember, to swarm is not to warn.

André Mangeot

WILD HONEY

Twisting the spoon in deep, you watch gold uncoil
into your porridge bowl where bees and butterflies
are lacquered round the rim. Beyond the glass
it's several summers since they buzzed and flitted
through our thistle-spotted grass, the back-meadow's
poppy, yarrow, lady's bedstraw. From even there
mites and parasites — varroa, wax moth, foulbrood —
have thinned them to a smatter and now with diggers,
ploughs and cutters three hedgerows in a day and
every flower goes under — another swathe of pasture
laid out for its bypass. And so, watched only by
the stars, pockets bursting, we steal out and scatter
through the night, packet after packet: red campion,
crested dogstail, birdsfoot trefoil, viper's bugloss.

John McCullough

THE ZIGZAG PATH

The day connives and you think you cannot live here,
in your body, alone and rushing forward all the time

like a silty river. All you wanted was to find a home
beside the souls of white roses and hurt no one

but the light keeps shifting. An invisible broom
keeps flicking you out from cover. You roll up

at each destination with a different face, as wrong
as the beech tree in Preston Park hung with trainers,

a museum of tongues. The day connives, but this dirt
is proof of trying. The chalk path you never longed for

zigzags through cowslips no one asked to throng.
In the park, a robin has built its nest inside a Reebok,

the shoe's throat packed with moss and a crooked
whisper of grass that says *I can, I can, I can.*

Kate Potts

GRIZZLY BEAR

[griz-lee bair]

n (pl grizzly bears)

1. *Ursus arctos horribilis.* A large North American brown; a wire-haired, silver-tipped, salmon-goading, spit-furred bear. Once widespread — now restricted.

2. A clumsy dance — part-zombie — in imitation of the tame, trained bear (*hist*), a dance to the side with a clunking, heavy step and little grace. The partners rear up, hands rigid and hooked as claws, as underworld song and dance, a degenerate act, a decided bending of the body that is wicked, scandalous, infamous and immoral, bawdy and obscene, corrupting the morals of the youth and public, ending all civilized modes of taste and seemliness — and too filthy, obscene and immoral to be in decency further described. These days, everybody's doing it.

3. A constellation, you remind me. We're stalled at a comfort-stop lay-by outside Mapperton — the engine's stewing gently, the sky a vapid darkness studded with white-hot plasma. And if it's a bear, it's a grizzly, silver tipped. You say *Lots of people talk to the animals. Not very many listen though.*

Melissa Studdard

TO BE WITH TREES

I dreamed of trees with blue veins in a forest full of wilting.
And there, all my southern girl self, full of *No thank yous*,

full of *You first* and *Go ahead and have the last piece of cake.*

I want that that last piece of cake. Dreamed the trees
made me my own torte, and I could have the whole thing.

My sisters, the trees, they said *Come now, sit, eat.*

They had blue veins in the forest full of wilting, and I cried.
There were no forks. They said my hands were fork enough.

And when I tried to say *please*, the trees said my eyes

were *please*, and they said my mouth was *thank you*,
and the trees cried too. They had beautiful eyes

for crying. A color I had never seen. So, I named it

Godlovesyoureyesbecauseshemadethemthisbeautifulcolor.
Now anyone who ever saw the color would think of the trees

and the meaning of the trees, which was to be.

Liz Berry

WHEN YOU TOUCH ME
I AM A WIND TURBINE

kaylied   birling blown blown   blown
until the atoms of the air cartwheel
around me like lindyhopping girls
i'm all surrender   all wow yes please
teasing the coy undergarments of the clouds
till they part their knees and rain o rain imbues
i'm unstoppable. topsy-turvy swinging
through the stars   arse tit toe

skyscrapers glow like birthday candles
and darkness whimpers in the city's gutters
when you   rough bluster   lay paws on me
a reeling silver whirl   spinning jenny
o give me your howl your squall   your fury
i'll make of it light and crackling blue beauty

Dom Bury

THRESHOLD

(for t.s and l.o)

And so we go now, as one
into the gathering darkness
not knowing how long the night will last
or how many terrored dreams
it may take to pass through these hours
or even if a different world will come at all
but destined to walk
as one humanity this road together.
And so we light our fires
and wait without hope together,
for hope would be hope of the wrong dawn.
And so we hold each other close
and wait without love
for love would be love of the wrong future.
Make no mistake this is the hour
where we rise or fall together.
This is the hour we face our own extinction
and choose whether we live or die together.
Yes, love, the timing is not of our choosing.
Yes, love, I too would want
to be born to another life than this.
And yet, in this same breath I know how
nothing has gone wrong,
been broken, thrown out of kilter.
That we have to be taken to the edge of death
to choose, as one, how we live.
This becomes then the most sacred of mirrors.
Will you stand by me in its dark glare awhile?
Will you feel me shudder and allow
yourself to fully shudder also?
All it asks of us to give up
is our unwillingness to surrender —
the fragile shrouds and masks we choose to wear,

to break open to ourselves, again, again.
This is for me the way forward now.
To keep on trusting
moment by moment
this feeling deep in my bones that says
out of the rubble of this one
a new world is going to come.
So if we need to be shown our collective death to come back
in the very nick of time
to life, to our collective love,
to understand what it means to be human
let it be so.

Anne Stevenson

NEAR THE END OF A DAY

Was that a butterfly
fluttering down to the grass
or a dead leaf?
A leaf, a leaf.
I can't see anywhere
the corpse of a butterfly.

Is that a white feather
asleep on the terrace
or a white cat's fur?
A feather, a feather
with a tiny grey caterpillar
curled at its root.

It is with such
questions and answers
near the end of a day
near the end of a summer
near the end of my life
that I reassure myself.

Nidhi Zak / Aria Eipe

WANDERSONG

some day, love, go into the wood,
and cast your sights out far ahead,
look closely for a flash of wand,
squint: conjuring of silver thread;
elbow emerged of feathered wing,
ribs stitched together inside out,
a goddess rising from the stream
skinkissed by darting silver trout.

race now, across the valley floor
footsparks that set a heart a-flame,
lie with her on the muddrunk floor,
and call this creature by her name:
sweet Caer that swanned into a girl
lakedrops still heavy in her hair
dripping over the fields she ran
caroling through the sunspun air.

some day, love, go out wandering
through this folk lore, these spirit lands
where whispered tell of tales long gone,
and fading light colours your hands;
pause there among the foxtail grass,
here: fix your wings, they've come undone,
and lift your shoulders to the moon,
and turn your face — full — to the sun.

ACKNOWLEDGEMENTS

Agodon, Kelli Russell, 'What I Call Erosion', *Dialogues with Rising Tides* (Copper Canyon Press, 2021).

Akhtar, Sascha, 'The Sufi', *Infinite Difference*, ed. Carrie Etter (Shearsman, 2010).

Ali, Kazim, 'Checkpoint', *Inquisition* (Wesleyan University Press, 2018).

Ali, Mir Mahfuz, 'MIG-21 Raids at Shegontola', *Midnight, Dhaka* (Seren, 2014).

Ameer, Abeer, 'The Storyteller', *Inhale/Exile* (Seren, 2021).

Armitage, Simon, 'I Kicked A Mushroom', *The Unaccompanied* (Faber, 2017).

Baker, David, 'Pastoral', *Swift* (Norton & Co, 2019).

Benson, Fiona, 'Eurofighter Typhoon', *Vertigo & Ghost* (Jonathan Cape, 2019).

Berry, Liz (2013) 'when you touch me i am a wind turbine', *Poetry Wales* 48.4.

Berry, Wendell, 'The Peace of Wild Things', *New Collected Poems* (Counterpoint, 2013).

Boast, Rachael, 'Agrarian Song', *Sidereal* (Picador, 2011).

Boland, Eavan, 'How We Were Transfigured', *The Historians* (Carcanet, 2020); *The Historians* (Norton, 2020).

Bonney, Sean, 'Our Death / What If the Summer Never Ends', *Our Death* (Commune Editions, 2019).

Boruch, Marianne, 'The Octopus', *The Anti-Grief* (Copper Canyon Press, 2019).

Burnett, Elizabeth-Jane, 'Llyn Gwynant', *Swims* (Penned in the Margins, 2017).

Burnside, John, 'Earth', *All One Breath* (Jonathan Cape, 2014).

Bury, Dom, 'Threshold', *Rite of Passage* (Bloodaxe, 2021).

Bush, Duncan, 'Couch Grass', *The Flying Trapeze* (Seren, 2012).

Campbell, Siobhán, 'The Longing of Bees', *Heat Signature* (Seren, 2017).

Capildeo, Vahni, 'The Pets of Others', *Venus As A Bear* (Carcanet, 2018).

Clarke, Gillian, 'Cantre'r Gwaelod', *Zoology* (Carcanet, 2017).

Cogan, Ross, 'Ragnarök', *Bragr* (Seren, 2018).

Davies, Grahame, 'Prayer', *Lightning Beneath the Sea* (Seren, 2012).

Doshi, Tishani, 'Self', *A God At the Door* (Bloodaxe, 2021).

Drake, Cath, 'How I Hold the World in This Climate Emergency', *The Shaking City* (Seren, 2020).

Dungy, Camille T, 'Trophic Cascade', *Trophic Cascade* (Wesleyan University Press, 2017).

Edwards, Rhian, 'The Gulls Are Mugging', *Brood* (Seren, 2017).

Etter, Carrie, 'Karner Blue', *The Weather in Normal* (Seren, 2018).

Francis, Vievee, 'Nightjar', *Forest Primeval* (Northwestern University Press, 2015).

Galleymore, Isabel, 'Limpet & Drill-Tongued Whelk', *Significant Other* (Carcanet, 2019).

Graham, W.S., 'I Leave This at Your Ear', *New Selected Poems* (Faber, 2018).

Groarke, Vona, 'The Riverbed', *Selected Poems* (Gallery, 2016).

Gross, Philip, 'The Floes', *Between the Islands* (Bloodaxe, 2020).

Gwyn, Richard, 'Taking Root', *Stowaway* (Seren, 2018).

Hadfield, Jen , 'Our Lady of Isbister', *Nigh No Place* (Bloodaxe, 2008).

Henry, Paul, 'Under the River', *Boy Running* (Seren, 2015).

Hewitt, Sean (2020) 'Meadow,' *Poetry Wales* 56.2.

Hicok, Bob (2018) 'Lush,' *Colorado Review* 45.3: 154-155.

Hicok, Bob, 'Lush', *Hold* (Copper Canyon, 2019).

Hirshfield, Jane, 'In A Kitchen Where Mushrooms Were Washed', *The Beauty*
      (Bloodaxe, 2015).

Hooson, Rhiannon, 'Thirlmere', *The Other City* (Seren, 2016).

Hunt, Jennifer (2001) 'September', *Poetry Wales* 37.3.

Jamie, Kathleen, 'The Creel', *Treehouse* (Picador, 2005).

Khalvati, Mimi, 'Eggs', *Afterwardness* (Carcanet, 2019).

Kinsella, John, 'Penillion of Cormorants in Polluted River', *Drowning in Wheat*
      (Picador, 2016).

Klink, Joanna, 'Some Feel Rain', *Raptus* (Penguin, 2010).

Lewis, Gwyneth, 'Pagan Angel', *Chaotic Angels* (Bloodaxe, 2005).

Loose, Gerry, 'After Amergin', *Antlers of Water,* ed. Kathleen Jamie (Cannongate,
      2019).

Lovell, Jane, 'Exhibit, "Song of Lost Species"', *This Tilting Earth* (Seren, 2019).

McCullough, John, 'The Zigzag Path', *Reckless Paper Birds* (Penned in the Margins,
      2019).

McGuckian, Medbh, 'The Colony Room', *Drawing Ballerinas* (Gallery Press,
2001); *The unfixed horizon : new selected poems* (Wake Forest, 2015).

Mangeot, André, 'Wild Honey', *Blood Rain* (Seren, 2020).

Meehan, Paula, 'Death of a Field', *Painting Rain* (Carcanet, 2009).

Militello, Jennifer, 'There Remain New Branches', *A Camouflage of Specimens and
      Garments* (Tupelo, 2016).

Miller, Kei, 'To Know Green From Green', *In Nearby Bushes* (Carcanet, 2019).

Minhinnick, Robert, 'The Magician', *Diary of the Last Man* (Carcanet, 2017).

Morley, David, 'Chorus, Enchantment' (Carcanet, 2010).

Naomi, Katrina, 'The Beach Couldn't Be Found', *Wild Persistence* (Seren, 2020)

Nezhukumatathil, Aimee, 'Invitation', *Oceanic* (Copper Canyon Press, 2018).

O'Reilly, Caitríona, 'A Brief History of Light', *The Nowhere Birds* (Bloodaxe, 2001).

Oswald, Alice, 'Seabird's Blessing', *Woods Etc* (Faber, 2011).

Petit, Pascale, 'For a Coming Extinction', *Tiger Girl* (Bloodaxe, 2020).

*Perez, Craig Santos, '(First Trimester)', from unincorporated territory [guma']
      (Omnidawn, 2017).*

Phillips, Carl , 'Monomoy', *Wild is the Wind* (Farrar Strauss & Giroux, 2018).

Pollard, Clare, 'In the Horniman Museum', *Incarnation* (Bloodaxe, 2017).

Potts, Kate, 'Grizzly Bear', *Feral* (Bloodaxe, 2018).

Pugh, Sheenagh, 'Visitor', *Afternoons Go Nowhere* (Seren, 2019).

Queyras, Sina, 'Endless Inter-States: 1', *Expressway* (Coach House Books, 2009).

Ravinthiran, Vidyan, 'More Context Required', *Gran-tu-molani* (Bloodaxe, 2014).

Rees-Jones, Deryn, 'Nightjar', *Erato* (Seren, 2019).

Revard, Carter, 'Over by Fairfax, Leaving Tracks', *An Eagle Nation* (University of Arizona Press, 1993).

Robinson, Roger, 'A Portable Paradise', *A Portable Paradise* (Peepaltree, 2019).

Robinsong, Erin, 'Late Prayer', *Rag Cosmology* (Book*hug Press, 2017).

Rumens, Carol, 'Easter Snow', *Animal People* (Seren, 2016).

Sheers, Owen, 'Liable to Floods', *Skirrid Hill* (Seren, 2005).

Shuttle, Penelope, 'The World Has Passed', *Unsent: New and Selected Poems 1980–2012* (Bloodaxe, 2012).

Simms, Colin, 'She is in the breaking of her seas', *Gyrfalcon Poems* (Shearsman, 2007).

Sirr, Peter, 'Whalefall', *The Rooms* (Gallery, 2014).

Sprackland, Martha (2015) 'Gone into the garden,' *The New Humanist* 130.2: 147.

Stevenson, Anne, 'At the end of the day', *Stone Milk* (Bloodaxe, 2007).

Strang, Em, 'Water of Ae', *Antlers of Water,* ed. Kathleen Jamie (Cannongate, 2019).

Stone, Will, 'The Extinction Plan', *Drawing In Ash* (Shearsman, 2015).

Symmons Roberts, Michael, 'A New Song', *Drysalter* (Jonathan Cape, 2013).

Szirtes, George, 'Climate', *Reel* (Bloodaxe, 2005).

Tamás, Rebecca, 'Witch Wood', *WITCH* (Penned in the Margins, 2019).

Thompson, Marvin, 'Whilst Searching for Anansi With My Mixed Race Children in the Blaen Bran Community Woodland', *Road Trip* (Peepal Tree Press, 2020).

Tongue, Samuel, 'Fish Counter', *Sacrifice Zones* (Red Squirrel Press, 2020).

van Neerven, Ellen, 'Love and Tradition', *Comfort Food* (University of Queensland Press, 2016).

Weise, The Cyborg Jillian, 'Body As Cloud', *The Amputee's Guide to Sex* (Soft Skull, 2017).

Westerman, Gwen Nell, 'Linear Process', *Follow the Blackbirds* (Michigan State University Press, 2013).

Wong, Jennifer, 'Yangtze', *Letters Home* (Nine Arches, 2020).

Yoseloff, Tamar, 'Knotweed', *A Formula for Night* (Seren, 2015).

BIOGRAPHIES

Gbenga Adesina, winner of the 2020 Narrative Prize, is a Nigerian writer and the author of the poetry chapbook, *Painter of Water*, a haunting meditation on art, language, and intimacy in the face of historical violence. His work has been published in *Harvard Review*, *Prairie Schooner*, the *New York Times*, and elsewhere.

Kelli Russell Agodon's most recent collection is *Dialogues with Rising Tides* (Copper Canyon Press). She's the cofounder of Two Sylvias Press and the Co-Director of Poets on the Coast. Agodon serves on the poetry faculty at the Rainier Writing Workshop, a low-residency MFA program at Pacific Lutheran University.

Sascha Aurora Akhtar originates from Pakistan and was educated there and in the USA. Her poetry collections include *#LoveLikeBlood, Whimsy of Dank Ju-Ju, 199 Japanese Names for Japanese Trees*, and *The Grimoire of Grimalkin* was greeted as "a contemporary masterpiece" by *The Guardian*. She also has a short fiction collection *Of Necessity & Wanting*. Her translations of feminist writer Hijab Imtiaz from the Indian Subcontinent are due in 2021 with Oxford University Press, India.

Kazim Ali has published numerous books of poetry, essays, and fiction, as well as cross-genre texts and translations of Marguerite Duras, Ananda Devi, and Sohrab Sepehri. He lives in San Diego and teaches at the University of California.

Mir Mahfuz Ali was born in Dhaka, Bangladesh. He studied at Essex and Cambridge Universities. He is the winner of the Geoffrey Dearmer Prize 2013. His first poetry collection, *Midnight, Dhaka*, was published in 2014 by Seren. He is now completing his second full collection.

Abeer Ameer's poems have appeared widely in publications including: *Acumen, Poetry Wales, Long Poem Magazine, Magma, Under the Radar* and *The Rialto*. Her debut poetry collection, *Inhale/Exile*, in which she shares stories of her Iraqi heritage, was published by Seren in February 2021.

Simon Armitage is the Poet Laureate. He has published twelve poetry collections, three best-selling volumes of non-fiction and he is a broadcaster, playwright and novelist. He has received numerous accolades including the Queens's Gold Medal for Poetry and the PEN Award for Poetry in Translation.

David Baker's new poetry volume, *Whale Fall*, will appear from W. W. Norton in 2022. Other books include *Swift: New and Selected Poems* (2019) and *Show Me Your Environment: Essays on Poetry, Poets, and Poems* (2014). He teaches at Denison University and is Poetry Editor of *Kenyon Review*.

Fiona Benson's collections are *Bright Travellers* and *Vertigo & Ghost*, which won the Forward Prize. Her third book *Ephemeron* is due out from Cape in 2022. She lives in mid-Devon with her husband and their two daughters.

Liz Berry is the author of *Black Country* (2014) and *The Republic of Motherhood* (2018), both from Chatto & Windus.

Wendell Berry is the author of over 50 books of poetry, fiction, and essays. He is a poet, novelist, and environmentalist and has maintained a farm for over 40 years in Port Royal, Kentucky. Among his many awards are the Ivan Sandrof Lifetime Achievement Award from the National Book Critics Circle, the T. S. Eliot Prize, and in 2010, he was awarded the National Humanities Medal by Barack Obama.

Rachael Boast (b. 1975) is a British poet and author of four collections, most recently, *Hotel Raphael* (Picador, 2021). She is co-editor of *The Echoing Gallery* (Redcliffe Press, 2013) and *The Caught Habits of Language* (Donut Press, 2018).

Born in Dublin in 1944, **Eavan Boland's** first book was published in 1967. A pioneering figure in Irish poetry, Boland's previous works include *The Journey and other poems* (1987), *Night Feed* (1994), *The Lost Land* (1998) and *Code* (2001). She divided her time between California and Dublin where she lived with her husband, the novelist Kevin Casey. Eavan died in Dublin on 27th April 2020.

Leo Boix is a bilingual Latinx poet born in Argentina who lives and works in the UK. Boix is a fellow of The Complete Works program and was the recipient of the Bart Wolffe Poetry Prize 2018 and the Keats-Shelley Prize 2019. *Ballad of a Happy Immigrant* (Chatto & Windus, 2021) is his debut English collection.

Sean Bonney (1969–2019) was a highly influential English poet, known for his engagement with political activism and progressive ideals. His poetry collections included *Our Death* (2019), the 2015 Verso Book of the Year *Letters Against the Firmament* (2016), *The Commons* (2011), *Blade Pitch Control Unit* (2005), and *Happiness: Poems After Rimbaud* (2011).

Marianne Boruch's 10th poetry collection is *The Anti-Grief* (Copper Canyon, 2019). *Bestiary Dark*, out in fall 2021, is based on her time as a Fulbright Scholar in Australia where she observed its astonishing wildlife. In 2018, she went rogue and emeritus from Purdue University where she taught for three decades.

Helen Bowell is a London-based poet and co-director of Dead [Women] Poets Society. She is a Ledbury Poetry Critic, and an alumna of The Writing Squad and the Roundhouse Poetry Collective. Her debut pamphlet is forthcoming from Bad Betty Press. She works at The Poetry Society.

Elizabeth-Jane Burnett is a writer and academic. Publications include *Of Sea*, *The Grassling: A Geological Memoir*, *Swims*, *A Social Biography of Contemporary Innovative Poetry Communities: the Gift, the Wager and Poethics*.

Jane Burn is a Pushcart/Forward Prize nominated, award-winning, neurodivergent poet, who lives in an off-grid wooden cottage in Northumberland. Her poems are widely published. Her next collection, *Be Feared*, will be published in November by Nine Arches Press. She is undertaking an MA in Writing Poetry at Newcastle University.

John Burnside lives and works in East Fife, where he teaches at the University of St Andrews. His new book, *Learning to Sleep*, is published by Jonathan Cape in August 2021.

Dom Bury is a devotee to this earth in this time of planetary transfiguration. He won The 2017 National Poetry Competition, The 2014 Magma Poetry Prize, 2nd Prize in The 2017 Resurgence Prize, has also received an Eric Gregory Award and a Jerwood/Arvon Mentorship. His first collection is *Rite of Passage* (Bloodaxe, 2021).

Duncan Bush (1946–2017) was a poet, novelist, dramatist, translator and documentary writer. He was born and brought up in Cardiff, Wales and his poetry collections *Aquarium* and *Salt* were both awarded the Welsh Arts Council Prize for Poetry. His collection *Masks* was a Poetry Book Society Recommendation and won the 1995 Arts Council of Wales 'Book of the Year' award.

Siobhán Campbell's latest collection is *Heat Signature* (Seren) — poems exploring intersections between natural and social worlds. Recent work appears in *Deep Time 2* (Black-Bough) and *Empty House* (Doire). On faculty at The Open University, Siobhan collaborates with activists to explore what creative writing can make happen, working in Northern Ireland, Lebanon and Iraq.

Vahni Capildeo's eight books and seven pamphlets include *Like a Tree, Walking* (Carcanet, 2021) and *Measures of Expatriation* (Carcanet, 2016), awarded the Forward Prize for Best Collection. Capildeo is Writer in Residence at the University of York, Visiting Scholar at Pembroke College, Cambridge, a Contributing Editor for *PN Review* and contributing adviser for *Blackbox Manifold*.

Gillian Clarke, National Poet of Wales 2008–2016. Recent publications: *Selected Poems*, Picador, 2016, *Zoology*, Carcanet, 2017, *Roots Home*, a collection of essays and a journal, 2021. Her version of the 7th century Welsh poem, *Y Gododdin*, was published by Faber, May 2021. In progress, *The Silence*, a collection of poems.

An Eric Gregory Award winner, **Ross Cogan** has published three collections, the most recent of which is *Bragr* (2018). One of the founders of the Cheltenham Poetry Festival, he was its Creative Director until 2019. Ross takes a keen interest in environmental matters and is semi-self-sufficient, growing most of his own vegetables, raising goats, ducks and chickens, and brewing mead.

Grahame Davies is a poet, novelist, editor and literary critic, who has won numerous prizes, including the Wales Book of the Year Award. He is the author of 18 books in Welsh and English, including: *The Chosen People*, a study of the relationship of the Welsh and Jewish peoples; *The Dragon and the Crescent*, a study of Wales and Islam; a novel, *Everything Must Change*, based on the life of the French philosopher Simone Weil, and two volumes of psychogeography, *Real Wrexham*, and *Real Cambridge*, published in 2021.

Tishani Doshi publishes poetry, essays and fiction. Her fourth full-length collection of poetry, *A God at the Door*, will be published by Bloodaxe Books and Copper Canyon Press in 2021. She lives in Tamil Nadu, India.

Cath Drake's collection *The Shaking City* (Seren Books), highly commended in the 2020 Forward Prizes, followed *Sleeping with Rivers*, a Poetry Book Society choice and winner of the Seren/Mslexia pamphlet prize. Australian born, Cath hosts The Verandah, online poetry teaching and events. She's an award-winning journalist with a specialism and post-graduate qualification in environmental science. https://cathdrake.com

Camille T. Dungy is the author of four collections of poetry, most recently *Trophic Cascade* (Wesleyan UP, 2017), winner of the Colorado Book Award, and a collection of personal essays *Guidebook to Relative Strangers* (W. W. Norton, 2017), a finalist for the National Book Critics Circle Award. Honors include a Guggenheim Fellowship in 2019. She has edited three anthologies, including *Black Nature* (University of Georgia). She is poetry editor for *Orion* and a University Distinguished Professor at Colorado State University.

Rhian Edward's first collection of poems *Clueless Dogs* (Seren, 2013) won Wales Book of the Year, the Roland Mathias Prize for Poetry, and Wales Book of the Year People's Choice. It was also shortlisted for the Forward Prize for Best First Collection. Rhian is also a winner of the John Tripp Award for Spoken Poetry, having won both the Judges and Audience award. Her eagerly awaited second collection *The Estate Agent's Daughter* is available now.

Originally from Normal, Illinois, **Carrie Etter** has published four collections of poetry, most recently *The Weather in Normal* (UK: Seren; US: Station Hill, 2018), a Poetry Book Society Recommendation. Her poems have appeared in *The Guardian*, *The New Republic*, *The Penguin Book of the Prose Poem*, and *The TLS*.

Sam Wilson Fletcher was born in Lewisham and studied at Oxford and Harvard. His poems have appeared in *Magma, Blackbox Manifold, Adjacent Pineapple, Die Leere Mitte* and elsewhere. Next summer he'll be poet-in-residence on board a boat exploring the Canadian Arctic.

Vievee Francis is the author of *Blue-Tail Fly* (Wayne State University Press, 2006), *Horse in the Dark* (Northwestern University Press, 2012), and *Forest Primeval* (Northwestern University Press, 2015), winner of the Kingsley Tufts Poetry Award and the Hurston / Wright Legacy Award for Poetry. She is an associate professor at Dartmouth College and an associate editor for *Callaloo*.

Isabel Galleymore's first collection, *Significant Other* (Carcanet), won the John Pollard Foundation International Poetry Prize in 2020 and was shortlisted for the Forward Best First Collection Prize. Her pamphlet, *Cyanic Pollens* (Guillemot Press), is based on her residency in the Peruvian Amazon. She lectures at the University of Birmingham.

Ross Gay is the author of four books of poetry: *Against Which; Bringing the Shovel Down; Be Holding*; and *Catalog of Unabashed Gratitude*, winner of the 2015 National Book Critics Circle Award and the 2016 Kingsley Tufts Poetry Award. His new poem, *Be Holding*, was released from the University of Pittsburgh Press in September 2020. His collection of essays, *The Book of Delights*, was released by Algonquin Books in 2019.

William Sydney Graham (1918–1986) was born in Greenock, Scotland. He trained as an engineer, before settling in Cornwall. He published seven collections of poetry, all of which can be found in *New Collected Poems* (Faber, 2004). *The Nightfisherman: Selected Letters of W.S. Graham* was published by Carcanet in 1999.

Irish poet **Vona Groarke** has published eleven books with The Gallery Press, of which the latest is *Double Negative* (2019). Her eighth collection, *Link*, is due in October 2021. She teaches part-time at the University of Manchester and otherwise lives in County Sligo in the West of Ireland.

Philip Gross has published some twenty collections of poetry, most recently *Between The Islands* (Bloodaxe, 2020). He is a keen collaborator — with poet Lesley Saunders on *A Part of the Main* (Mulfran, 2018) and with Welsh-language poet Cyril Jones and artist Valerie Coffin Price on the bilingual *Troeon/Turnings* (Seren, 2021). www.philipgross.co.uk

Richard Gwyn is a Welsh poet, novelist and translator. His memoir, *The Vagabond's Breakfast*, won a Wales Book of the Year award in 2012. His work has appeared in over a dozen languages. He is the author of Ricardo Blanco's Blog. *Stowaway: A Levantine Adventure* (2018) is published by Seren.

Jen Hadfield's poetry is published by Picador. Her fourth collection, *The Stone Age*, explores neurodiversity which came out in March 2021. She is also working on *Storm Pegs*, a collection of essays about Shetland, where she lives.

Paul Henry's books include *The Brittle Sea: New & Selected Poems, Boy Running* and *Ingrid's Husband*. Originally a songwriter, he's performed his poems and songs at festivals in Europe, Asia and the USA. He's guest-edited *Poetry Wales* and presented arts programmes for BBC Radio Wales, Radio 3 and Radio 4.

Seán Hewitt lectures at Trinity College Dublin and is a Book Critic for The Irish Times. *Tongues of Fire* (Cape, 2020), his debut collection of poetry, was shortlisted for The Sunday Times Young Writer of the Year 2020, the John Pollard Foundation International Poetry Prize, 2021, and the Dalkey Literary Award, 2021.

Bob Hicok's tenth collection is *Red Rover Red Rover* (2021). A two-time finalist for the National Book Critics Circle Award and recipient of the Bobbitt Prize from the Library of Congress, he's also been awarded a Guggenheim, two NEA Fellowships, and nine Pushcart Prizes.

Jane Hirshfield's most recent poetry collection, *Ledger* (Knopf and Bloodaxe, 2020), centers on the crises of biosphere and social justice. Her work appears in *The TLS, The New York Times, The Guardian,* and *Poetry*. In 2019, she was inducted into the American Academy of Arts & Sciences.

Rhiannon Hooson has won major awards for her work, including an Eric Gregory Award from the Society of Authors, and her first book was shortlisted for the Wales Book of the Year award. She has been featured in the *Guardian, Magma,* and *Poetry Wales,* and has recently been a Literature Wales bursary recipient, Hay Festival Writer at Work, and judge of the PENfro festival poetry competition.

Jennifer Hunt is an artist and nature writer living in a medieval thatched cottage in Dorset. She graduated with an MA in Creative Writing from Bath Spa University in 2001. Since then, her environmental poetry has been published in several anthologies and magazines. Her writing is regularly successful in competitions.

Kathleen Jamie is a poet and essayist. Her poetry collections have won the Somerset Maugham Award, the Geoffrey Faber Memorial Prize, the Forward Poetry Prize, the Costa Poetry Award and Saltire Book of the Year. Her three essay collections include *Sightlines* which won the Orion Book Award in the USA.

Born in Tehran, Iran, and resident in London, **Mimi Khalvati** has published numerous poetry collections, including *The Meanest Flower*, shortlisted for the T.S. Eliot Prize 2007, *Child: New and Selected Poems 1991–2011*, a Poetry Book Society Special Commendation and, most recently, *Afterwardness*, a book of the year in *The*

Sunday Times and *The Guardian*. Her awards include a Cholmondeley Award from the Society of Authors, a major Arts Council Writer's Award, and she is the founder of the Poetry School, a Fellow of the Royal Society of Literature and of The English Society.

John Kinsella's recent volumes of poetry include *Drowning in Wheat: Selected Poems* (Picador, 2016) and *Brimstone: a book of villanelles* (Arc, 2020). His new memoir is *Displaced* (Transit Lounge, 2020). He is a Fellow of Churchill College, Cambridge, and Emeritus Professor of Literature and Environment at Curtin University.

Joanna Klink is the author of five books of poetry, most recently *The Nightfields* (Penguin 2020). She has received awards and fellowships from the American Academy of Arts and Letters, the Trust of Amy Lowell, and the Guggenheim Foundation. She teaches at the Michener Center for Writers in Austin, Texas.

Gwyneth Lewis was National Poet of Wales 2005–2006 and wrote the six-foot-high words on the front of the iconic Wales Millennium Centre. She's published nineteen books, including poetry, non-fiction, plays, novellas. Her latest publication is a translation, with Rowan Williams, of the *Book of Taliesin* (Penguin Classics).

Gerry Loose is a poet living on the Isle of Bute who works with subjects from the natural world, most specifically with plants, as well as in the world of geo-politics. His work is found inscribed and created in Parks, Botanic Gardens and in natural landscapes, galleries, hospitals as well as on the page. His most recent book is *The Great Book of the Woods*.

Jane Lovell is an award-winning British poet whose work focuses on our relationship with the planet and its wildlife. Her latest collection is the prize-winning *God of Lost Ways* (Indigo Dreams Press). Jane also writes for *Dark Mountain*, *Photographers Against Wildlife Crime* and *Elementum Journal*. She lives in Kent and is Writer-in-Residence at Rye Harbour Nature Reserve.

John McCullough lives in Hove. His most recent book of poems, *Reckless Paper Birds* (Penned in the Margins) won the 2020 Hawthornden Prize for Literature and was shortlisted for the Costa Poetry Award. His collections have been named Books of the Year in *The Independent*, *The Guardian* and *The Observer*.

Medbh McGuckian is an influential poet, born in 1950 in Belfast where she continues to live. She has been Writer-in-Residence at Queen's University, Belfast, the University of Ulster, Coleraine, and Trinity College, Dublin, and was Visiting Fellow at the University of California, Berkeley. She is author of numerous poetry collections, most recently *Marine Cloud Brightening* (2019, shortlisted for the 2020 *Irish Times* Poetry Now Award).

André Mangeot's collections are *Natural Causes* (2003), *Mixer* (2005) and *Blood Rain* (Seren, 2020) along with two books of short stories, *A Little Javanese* and *True North* (Salt, 2008 & 2010). He lives in Cambridge and has worked in the charity fundraising sector for over twenty years. www.andremangeot.com

Paula Meehan was born in Dublin where she still lives. She has published five previous collections of poetry and received many awards for her work, including the Denis Devlin Award of the Irish Arts Council (An Chomhairle Ealaíon) for *Dharmakaya* which Carcanet published in 2000.

Jennifer Militello is the author of *The Pact* (Tupelo Press/Shearsman Books, 2021) and the memoir *Knock Wood*, winner of the Dzanc Nonfiction Prize (Dzanc Books, 2019), as well as four additional collections of poetry. She teaches in the MFA program at New England College.

Kei Miller was born in Jamaica in 1978 and is an award-winning poet, novelist and essayist. His 2014 collection, *The Cartographer Tries to Map a Way to Zion*, won the Forward Prize for Best Collection while his 2017 Novel, *Augustown*, won the Bocas Prize for Caribbean Literature.

Robert Minhinnick is co-founder of Friends of the Earth Cymru and the charity Sustainable Wales/Cymru Gynaliadwy. Editor of *Gorwelion/Shared Horizons* from Parthian Books, 2021. His next volume is *The Extinction Circus*, Seren 2022.

David Morley won the Ted Hughes Award for *The Invisible Gift*. His latest poetry collection *FURY* was a Poetry Book Society Choice and was shortlisted for the Forward Prize for best collection. He is a Fellow of The Royal Society of Literature.

Katrina Naomi received an Authors' Foundation award from the Society of Authors for work on her third collection, *Wild Persistence* (Seren, 2020). Her second poetry collection, *The Way the Crocodile Taught Me*, was chosen by Foyles Bookshop as one of its Foyles' Five for Poetry. Her debut collection *The Girl with the Cactus Handshake* received an Arts Council Award. Katrina's recent work has been broadcast on Radio 4's *Front Row*, *Poetry Please*, BBC TV *Spotlight* and on Poems on the Underground.

Aimee Nezhukumatathil is the author of the book of nature essays, *World of Wonders*, and four collections of poetry. A Guggenheim and NEA fellow, she is professor of English at University of Mississippi.

Caitríona O'Reilly's first collection *The Nowhere Birds* was shortlisted for the Forward Prize for Best First Collection in 2001, and won the Rooney Prize for Irish Literature in 2002. Her second collection, *The Sea Cabinet* (Bloodaxe Books, 2006), was a Poetry Book Society Recommendation and shortlisted for the *Irish Times* Poetry Now Award in 2007. Her third, *Geis* (Bloodaxe Books, UK; Wake Forest University

Press, USA, 2015), won the *Irish Times* Poetry Now Award 2016, was shortlisted for the Pigott Poetry Prize, and was a Poetry Book Society Recommendation.

Alice Oswald studied Classics at Oxford and then trained as a gardener. She worked in gardens for seven years before publishing her first book of poems, *The Thing In The Gap-Stone Stile*, which won the Forward Prize in 1996. Other collections have won the inaugural Ted Hughes award, the Hawthornden prize, the Warwick prize, and the Costa Poetry Award. In 2009 she won a Cholmondeley award for her contribution to poetry, and in 2017 she won the International Griffin Poetry Prize. She is married with three children and lives in Devon.

Craig Santos Perez is an indigenous Pacific Islander poet from Guam. He is the author of five collections of poetry and the co-editor of five anthologies. He teaches at the University of Hawai'i at Manoa.

Pascale Petit's eighth collection, *Tiger Girl* (Bloodaxe Books, 2020), was shortlisted for the Forward Prize, and a poem from the book won the Keats-Shelley Prize. Her previous collection, *Mama Amazonica* (Bloodaxe Books, 2017), won the inaugural Laurel Prize 2020 and the RSL Ondaatje Prize 2018. Four of her collections were shortlisted for the T.S. Eliot Prize.

Carl Phillips's new book, *Then the War and Selected Poems, 2007–2020* will be out in 2022 from Farrar, Straus & Giroux in the US and from Carcanet in the UK. Phillips teaches at Washington University in Saint Louis, Missouri.

Clare Pollard has published five collections of poetry with Bloodaxe, most recently *Incarnation.* She edits *Modern Poetry in Translation.* Her latest book is a non-fiction title, *Fierce Bad Rabbits: The Tales Behind Children's Picture Books* (Penguin).

Kate Potts' second collection, *Feral*, was a Poetry Book Society recommendation and a *Telegraph* poetry book of the month. She teaches creative writing for Middlesex University and the Poetry School.

Sheenagh Pugh still thinks of herself as a Welsh poet but now lives in Shetland. She has published many poetry collections: her latest is *Afternoons Go Nowhere* (Seren, 2019).

Sina Queyras is the author most recently of *My Ariel*, *Mx'l* and *Expressway*, all from Coach House Books.

Vidyan Ravinthiran is the author of two collections: *The Million-Petalled Flower of Being Here* (Bloodaxe, 2019) was a Poetry Book Society Recommendation. He has also written an award-winning study of Elizabeth Bishop. He teaches at Harvard University.

Deryn Rees-Jones's most recent book of poems is *Erato* (Seren 2019). She teaches at the University of Liverpool.

Carter Revard is a professor emeritus of English at Washington University, and he lives in St. Louis. Revard is the author of the poetry collections *Ponca War Dances* (1980), *Cowboys and Indians Christmas Shopping* (1992), and *An Eagle Nation* (1993), as well as the nonfiction collection *Family Matters, Tribal Affairs* (1998) and a memoir in prose and poetry, *Winning the Dust Bowl* (2001).

Roger Robinson is the winner of the T.S. Eliot Prize 2019 and RSL Ondaatje Prize 2020, shortlisted for the Derek Walcott Prize for Poetry 2020 and the OCM Bocas Poetry Prize.

Erin Robinsong is a poet and interdisciplinary artist working with ecological imagination. Her debut collection of poetry, *Rag Cosmology*, won the 2017 A.M. Klein Prize for Poetry, and her chapbooks include *Liquidity* (House House Press, 2020). Her work has appeared in *Lemon Hound, The Capilano Review, Effects, Regreen: New Canadian Ecological Poetry*, and many others. Originally from Cortes Island, Erin lives in Montréal, Canada.

Carol Rumens's latest collection of poems is *The Mixed Urn* (Sheep Meadow, 2019, USA). She has published several collections with Seren, including *Blind Spots* and *Animal People*. She lives in Gwynedd and is a Professor Emerita of Creative Writing at Bangor University.

Owen Sheers is a novelist, poet and playwright. His BAFTA and Grierson nom-inated film-poem, *The Green Hollow* has recently been published by Faber, who also published his BBC film-poem to mark the 70th anniversary of the NHS, *To Provide All People*. He is Professor in Creativity at Swansea University.

Penelope Shuttle's new collection, *Lyonesse,* appears from Bloodaxe, June 2021. *Covid/Corvid*, a pamphlet written in collaboration with Alyson Hallett, appears from Broken Sleep Books, November 2021. *Father Lear*, a pamphlet, was published by Poetry Salzburg in June 2020. *Conversations on a Bench* was broadcast on BBC Radio 4 in March 2020.

Colin Simms—poet, naturalist, and lifelong independent observer—was born in 1939, and lives as an author and freelance naturalist in the North of England. He is not an orthodox conservationist, but insists on the privacy, 'isness', for wildlife which modern trends deny. He has published thousands of natural-history letters, articles, reports, scientific notes and papers, broadcasts and (above all) poems, and his scientific work has an international reputation.

Peter Sirr has published ten poetry collections, of which the most recent are *The Gravity Wave* (2019), a Poetry Book Society recommendation, and *Sway* (2016). *The Rooms* (2014) was shortlisted for the Irish Times Poetry Now Award and the Pigott Poetry Prize. *The Thing Is* (2009) was awarded the Michael Hartnett Prize in 2011. He lives in Dublin.

Martha Sprackland is an editor, writer and translator from Merseyside. Previously poetry editor for *Poetry London*, she is also founder–editor of Offord Road Books. Martha's debut collection, *Citadel*, was shortlisted for the Costa Poetry Prize, the Forward Prize for Best First Collection and the John Pollard International Poetry Prize.

Anne Stevenson (1933-2020) was born in Cambridge, England, of American parents, and grew up in New England and Michigan. After several transatlantic switches, she settled in Britain in 1964. As well as her numerous collections of poetry, Anne Stevenson published a biography of Sylvia Plath (1989), a book of essays, *Between the Iceberg and the Ship* (1998), and two critical studies of Elizabeth Bishop's work, most recently *Five Looks at Elizabeth Bishop* (2006).

Em Strang is a poet, novelist, mentor and founder of Scottish charity, Three Streams, offering workshops and retreats in creativity, contemplation & landwork. Em's writing preoccupations are with nature, Christian mysticism and the relationship between the human and nonhuman. https://em-strang.co.uk

Will Stone is a poet, literary translator and essayist. His most recent collection is *The Slowing Ride* (Shearsman, 2020). His debut *Glaciation* (Salt 2007) won a major international poetry prize. In 2021, new poems have appeared in the *Spectator*, the *London Magazine*, *Agenda*, *Poetry Review* and *London Grip*. Pushkin Press published his *Collected Poems of Georg Trakl* in 2019 and *Poems to Night* by Rilke in 2020.

Melissa Studdard is the author of the poetry collection *I Ate the Cosmos for Breakfast*. Her work has been featured by PBS, NPR, *The New York Times*, *The Guardian*, and more. She is the 2020 winner of the Lucille Medwick Award from the Poetry Society of America. www.melissastuddard.com.

Michael Symmons Roberts is a poet and novelist who has worked as a newspaper journalist, a BBC radio producer, a documentary filmmaker, and collaborated with musical composers. He won the Whitbread Poetry Award, the Forward Prize and the Costa Poetry Prize. He is Professor of Poetry at Manchester Metropolitan University.

George Szirtes's twelfth book of poems, *Reel* (2004) won the T.S. Eliot Prize for which he has been twice shortlisted since. His latest is *Mapping the Delta* (2016). His memoir *The Photographer at Sixteen* was awarded the James Tait Black Prize in 2020.

Rebecca Tamás is the author of the poetry collection *WITCH* (Penned in the Margins, 2019), and the essay collection *Strangers: Essays on the Human and Nonhuman* (Makina Books, 2020). She is a lecturer in Creative Writing at York St John University.

Marvin Thompson was born in London to Jamaican parents and now lives in mountainous south Wales. He is the winner of the Poetry Society's National Poetry Competition, 2020. He was the first poet of colour to win since 1981. His debut poetry collection, *Road Trip* (Peepal Tree Press, 2020), is a Poetry Book Society Recommendation.

Samuel Tongue's first collection of poetry, *Sacrifice Zones*, was published by Red Squirrel in 2020. He has published two pamphlets: *Hauling-Out* (Eyewear, 2016) and *Stitch* (Tapsalteerie, 2018). His poems have appeared in *Butcher's Dog, Magma, The Compass, Finished Creatures, Gutter, The Interpreter's House* and elsewhere. samueltongue.com

Of Mununjali Yugambeh (South East Queensland) and Dutch heritage, **Ellen van Neerven** writes fiction, poetry, plays and non-fiction. They received numerous awards for their first book, *Heat and Light*, as well as their two poetry collections, the most recent *Throat*, winning the Kenneth Slessor Prize for Poetry, the Multicultural NSW Award and Book of the Year in the NSW Premier's Literary Awards.

Maggie Wang is an undergraduate at the University of Oxford, where she leads the Oxford University Poetry Society. Her writing has appeared in *Ruminate, Not Very Quiet, perhappened mag,* and others. She is also a 2021 Ledbury Emerging Poetry Critic. When not writing, she enjoys playing the piano and exploring nature.

The Cyborg Jillian Weise is a poet, video artist and disability rights activist. Her 4th book, *Cyborg Detective* (BOA Editions, 2019) won the PEN Oakland Josephine Miles Award.

Gwen Nell Westerman's poems, essays, and short stories appear in numerous publications, including the *Norton Anthology of Native Nations Poetry* (2020); the Minnesota issue of *Quiltfolk* (January 2020); and *New Poets of Native Nations* (Graywolf Press, 2018). Her poetry collection *Follow the Blackbirds* (2013) was published by Michigan State University Press.

Writer and translator **Jennifer Wong** was born and grew up in Hong Kong and now lives in the UK. Her new collection, 回家 *Letters Home*, published by Nine Arches Press in 2020, has been named a Wild Card choice by Poetry Book Society. She is also the author of *Goldfish* (Chameleon Press, 2013) — which won the Hong Kong Arts Development Council Young Artist Award (Literary Arts) and a pamphlet, *Diary of a Miu Miu Salesgirl* (Bitter Melon Poetry, 2019).

Tamar Yoseloff's sixth collection is *The Black Place* (Seren, 2019). She's also the author of *Formerly* (with photographs by Vici MacDonald), shortlisted for the Ted Hughes Award, and collaborative editions with artists Linda Karshan and Charlotte Harker respectively. She's a lecturer on the Poetry School / Newcastle University MA in Writing Poetry.

Nidhi Zak/Aria Eipe is a poet, pacifist and fabulist. Founder of the Play It Forward Fellowships, she is poetry editor at Skein Press and Fallow Media and contributing editor with *The Stinging Fly*. Her debut poetry collection, *Auguries of a Minor God*, is forthcoming from Faber & Faber.

The Editors

Zoë Brigley has three Poetry Book Society recommended poetry collections: *The Secret* (2007), *Conquest* (2012), and *Hand & Skull* (2019) (all from Bloodaxe). She recently published a poetry chapbook, *Aubade After A French Movie* (Broken Sleep 2020) and has another forthcoming: *Into Eros* (Verve, 2021). She has a collection of nonfiction essays *Notes from a Swing State* (Parthian, 2019). She is Assistant Professor in English at the Ohio State University where she produces an anti-violence podcast: *Sinister Myth*. She won an Eric Gregory Award for the best British poets under 30, was Forward Prize commended, and listed in the Dylan Thomas Prize. She is co-editor (with Kristian Evans) of the Seren anthology *100 Poems to Save the Earth*.

Kristian Evans is a poet and editor from Kenfig in south Wales, interested in ecological philosophy, magic and receptions of the more-than-human. He has written several texts for performance as well as chapbooks of poems and nonfiction, *Unleaving* (HappenStance, 2016), and *Otherworlds* (Broken Sleep, 2021). He is also an amateur naturalist, with a particular interest in sand dune ecology.